I just finished reading SHOAH: *Journey from the Ashes*.

For the past 25 years I have read an average of two Holocaust books per week. I have read good books, bad books, mediocre books, and some outstanding books. This book I would gladly recommend to anyone to read as it goes beyond the Holocaust and goes to humanity.

Cantor Fettman mixes in sociology, psychology, common sense, and his experiences taking him from faith to faith never with a loss for where G-d is in his life.

I am proud that Cantor Fettman was one of the 60 interviews that I conducted for the Spielberg Survivors of the Shoah Visual History Foundation. He is a man that leaves an impact. He is a man who has made a difference.

This book is well written with just enough reference to the Holocaust to be a Holocaust book and, at the same time, this book becomes a primer on how to live your life.

I dare to dream for a moment thinking how this world would be if in each person's life a Cantor Fettman appeared. It also leaves that void wondering how many Cantor Fettmans were murdered during the Holocaust.

This book should be required reading for everyone at any age and with any religion.

I would tell anyone searching for a book on the Holocaust to begin right here.

Ben Nachman, DDS
Omaha, NE

Leo Fettman

A letter received from Paul M. Lundell, D.D.
Pastor Emeritus

When I came to Omaha to serve as Pastor of Dundee Presbyterian Church, one of the first clergy-neighbors I met was Cantor Leo Fettman who had come to Omaha several years earlier. As we became acquainted and shared our life stories, I came to realize how sheltered my life had been even though our family had been through the Depression of the 1930s.

In March 1944, when young Fettman and his family had ten minutes to leave their home by order of the Nazis, I was cheering for our basketball team and soon to earn some pocket money cutting grass. In April of that year, in the cattle car on their way to death at Auschwitz, some of the men with him sang psalms even as we did in my home church. He lost his parents, brother and sister, while I enjoyed my folks and my home. What a contrast, the mid 1940s for him and for me!

I came to realize how sheltered were the lives of my Confirmation Class pupils. None had known poverty. They knew little or nothing about the reality of evil in this world. So I invited Cantor Fettman to tell his story to them. In the same quiet way in which *SHOAH* was written, he told them about his firsthand experience in the Holocaust.

We continued this throughout the years I served before my retirement. Cantor Fettman seemed to understand their sheltered existence and how to get them to see the reality of evil as he had experienced it. Almost all my Confirmands responded to his presentation thoughtfully, reflectively. He made a valuable contribution to their lives.

For much the same reason, I recommend *SHOAH: Journey from the Ashes* to all who would try to comprehend the human cost of anti-Semitism and the Holocaust.

Paul M. Lundell, D.D.
Pastor Emeritus

Leo Fettman

SHOAH

JOURNEY FROM THE ASHES

A Personal Story of
Triumph Over the Holocaust

by
CANTOR LEO FETTMAN
As told to Paul M. Howey

Illustrations by
Annette Sherman Fettman

Published 1999 by
Six Points Press, Inc.
Omaha, NE USA

Produced by
Five Star Publications, Inc.
P.O. Box 6698
Chandler, AZ 85246-6698

Six Points Press, Inc.
P.O. Box 31421 • Omaha, Nebraska 68131-0421

Holocaust Photos courtesy of Documentary Photo Aids, Inc.
POB 952137 Lake Mary, FL 32795

Library of Congress Cataloging-in-Publication Data

Fettman, Leo, 1925-

Shoah: journey from the ashes : a personal story of triumph over the
Holocaust / by Leo Fettman as told to Paul M. Howey ;
Illustrations by Annette Sherman Fettman. –1st ed.

p.   Cm

ISBN 0-9679721-0-8

1. Fettman, Leo, 1925- .
2. Jews - Hungary - Nyíradony - Biography.
3. Holocaust, Jewish (1939-1945) - Hungary - Nyíradony-
   Personal narratives.
4. Holocaust survivors - Nebraska - Omaha - Biography.
5. Nyíradony (Hungary) - Biography.
6. Omaha (Neb.) - Biography. I. Howey, Paul II. Title.

DS135.H93F47 1999
940.53'18'092-dc21
[B]   98-50073
                                                 CIP

Publishing Consultant: Linda F. Radke/Five Star Publications, Inc.
Illustrations: Annette Sherman Fettman
Cover, layout, book design: Lynlie Hermann/Five Star Publications, Inc.
Proofreader: Gail Baker/Five Star Publications, Inc.
Typesetting: T. G. Haynes/Five Star Publications, Inc.

Dedication

In memory of my dear beloved parents, Yaakov and Feige Esther Fettman; my grandmother, Hinda Weisz; my sister, Margit; Margit's three children, Binyamin Aryeh, Tzvi, and Leah; my brother, Sandor; and the many other members of our family who were murdered by the Nazis.

I thank my beloved parents for imbuing me with Torah Judaism. Unfortunately, they were torn away from us and did not live to enjoy *yiddishe nachas* from their children, grandchildren, and great-grandchildren.

Cantor Leo Fettman

פטטמן

יעקב בן בנימין אריה ע"ה
ואשתו
פיינע אסתר בת אליעזר ע"ה

הם נרצחו על ידי הנאצים
הרוצחים הגרמנים
ימח שמם וזכרם
באושוויץ

כ"ג אייר תש"ד

ת.נ.צ.ב.ה.

Acknowledgments

I am most thankful to my G-d* who spared my life and directed me toward the fulfillment of certain missions.

I wish to thank Bob Wolfson, director of the Anti-Defamation League in Omaha, Nebraska, who joins me in the fight against bigotry and anti-Semitism. I must acknowledge my friend, Lynda Mirvish, who assisted in editing my early notes and for providing encouragement. I sincerely thank those members of my audience who came forward to urge me to record my story.

I thank my brother, Dezso, and his wife, Margie, for helping me recall events and names from the past. Most certainly, I am very grateful to my wife, Annette, for her support and assistance in this endeavor. She had a major share in all aspects of this book's publication. I most appreciate her translating my "Hungarian English" into "American English" and her ability to navigate me on the highways to the many communities where I am asked to speak.

Lastly, I must thank my family for putting up with my survivor's temperament.

---

* According to Jewish tradition, to write out the name of the Supreme Being in full turns the text into a sacred scripture. In this book, therefore, His name will be spelled G-d.

Contents

Foreword

In April 1994, Yoni Schwab, Cantor Fettman's seventeen-year-old grandson, went on the "March of the Living," a program that takes Jewish teenagers from around the world to Poland where they visit concentration camps. Yoni delivered this speech before his congregation at Temple Sinai in Middletown, New York, two weeks after returning home.

I recently visited the concentration camps, the ghettos, witnessed what's left of Jewish life in Poland, and commemorated *Yom HaShoah* (Holocaust Remembrance Day).

My grandfather, a survivor of Auschwitz, inspired me to attempt the trip. The journey has given me a mission. As I left to return home, I wanted to tell everyone what I had seen, to communicate the Holocaust to the whole world. My challenge came in finding the proper words. I found I could relate individual incidents to people who asked, but I could not tell the whole story. I found myself prefacing my comments with: "There are some experiences I had and emotions I felt that I cannot put into words."

I wish I could describe the look on the face of Mr. Mayer, a Hungarian survivor of Auschwitz, as he reentered his block in Auschwitz, Block 18, for the first time since the war; or words to capture the emotion in his voice as he read the Kaddish (the prayer for the dead) in a gas chamber in Auschwitz almost exactly fifty years after his family perished there. How can I describe my emotions upon entering Barracks 11 and seeing the three tiers of bare, wooden slats no wider than my dining room table that held up to ten barely live skeletons apiece? Frantically, I ran around inside the barracks, counting the sets of tiered bunk beds. I needed to know how many had been kept there. Assuming ten people per bunk, how many people did the Nazis squeeze under one roof? In a daze, I counted bunks.

I walked and counted, walked and counted, determined I would not let my emotions catch up with me. Fifty-two. Fifty-two sets of three-tiered bunks, each holding ten people. In all, 1,560 human beings. And the bunk over there — yes, that one. Could it have held my grandfather? Or maybe it was that one. Who could tell?

How can I describe Treblinka? The camp is gone. Only a memorial remains in its place. The memorial ignores individuals. Instead, it represents the communities. In all, 17,000 stones large and small, cover an enormous field. Each stone represents one community lost, perished, disappeared, its inhabitants murdered. Only 180 of the larger stones bear names of communities. The largest reads simply: "Warsaw." I did not spend my time at that one. I could not comprehend the magnitude of the hundreds of thousands of Jews it memorialized. Rather, I was drawn to the smallest stone. No larger than a football and not at all impressive-looking, it represented a nameless *shtetl* (village) and its fifty victims. The smallest, most insignificant rock had the impossible task of memorializing fifty lives.

Majdanek. What words can properly communicate the horrors of that death camp? How can I describe the emotions that bombarded me as I stared at a barracks filled with nothing but shoes? What about the second barracks filled with shoes? Or the third? Intellectually, I can understand six million, but emotionally, I could only begin to grasp it. How can I share the despair and the energy of so many teenagers in a circle, holding hands, singing *Od Avinu Hai* (*Our Father is Still Alive*) in the middle of Field 3 of the Majdanek death camp?

When I entered the main gas chamber complex at Majdanek, my emotions took over. I could no longer "think" about what I was seeing. How many died here? When I saw the dissection table, I dared not imagine what was done to the victims. All of that was far from my mind, yet I could feel the weight of each one of them on my shoulders.

I felt frustration and anger over my *Yahrzeit* (Memorial) candle. Dozens of these candles glowed solemnly around a pile of bones in the center of the next room of the gas chamber. Why was mine the only one that refused to be lit? Then I entered the crematorium. People stood. People looked. People cried. I saw boys my age, nearly men, still at the macho age, break down like babies, turning their eyes away from the ovens. I saw a boy I barely knew was looking, too. We hugged each other without speaking. I needed the support and so did he. I wanted to cry. I wanted to let my emotions free. I wanted to let the world know that I cared. But I could not cry. My emotions were trapped within me, where they remain today. I hope that people will hear me speak, and they will cry. And when they cry over the Holocaust, then they will cry for me as well. That will happen, however, only when I find the words to describe what is deep down inside me.

My experiences came together at Yad VaShem, Israel's Holocaust Museum in Jerusalem, where I rushed through the exhibits to reach the area most important to me. In the museum, there is a large copy of a picture of the "selection" at Auschwitz. The picture is of my grandfather's father and brother. A wider-angle lens would have captured my grandfather, who was standing with them. I stood there for a long time, overcome by emotion. I looked at the date on the picture: April 15, 1944. I stood before it on April 13, 1994.

You have come to hear the stories, to learn about the Holocaust, and I have done my best to share my experiences with you. If it is difficult to relate them to you, how much more so it is to reach the rest of the world? You are the ones who want to hear, but what about the ones who don't want to listen?

Historical Prologue

The story of Cantor Leo Fettman's youth in Hungary and of his experiences at the hands of the Nazis is a tragic and poignant tale, yet it is but the blink of an eye in the centuries-old and venerable history of the Jews. To better grasp the nuances of his tale, it is important to place them in the context of world and religious history.

In the Beginning

In the earliest years following the preachings of Christ, Christianity was essentially just another branch of Judaism, with the two groups even sharing synagogues. The gentile churches were led by Paul of Tarsus and the Jewish sect (the Ebionites) by James, the brother of Christ. While there was competition between the two groups, primarily for converts, there was neither prejudice nor violence. This spirit of cooperation, however, was not destined to last.

The Christians began distancing themselves from the Judaic dietary laws and the requirement for circumcision. Eventually, it became politically expedient for them to alleviate the blame of the Romans for the crucifixion, and so they gradually shifted the onus to the Jews. Thus labeled as the killers of Christ, the Jews were further ostracized for refusing to accept Christ as the messiah. Selected scriptures were offered as evidence that the Jews had broken the covenant with G-d and were cast as a wicked people. Anti-Semitism, by whatever name, became an interwoven part of early Christian beliefs.

Following two revolutions (66-70 and 133-135), thousands of Jews emigrated from their homelands to various parts of Europe. In 313, Constantine the Great issued the Edict of Milan naming Christianity the official religion of the Roman empire, and those who helped found the new state church took to the pulpit to further excoriate the Jews. Catholic theologian and Bishop of Hippo St. Augustine (354-430) wrote:

> The true image of the Hebrew is Judas Iscariot, who sells the Lord for silver. The Jew can never understand the Scriptures and forever will bear the guilt for the death of Jesus.

St. Augustine's words proved not to be an aberration in Christian history, but rather a harbinger of events to come over the succeeding centuries. Still, a Jewish society of community councils, synagogues, and academies began to flourish, a fact that did not go unrecognized by the Christian leaders. In an effort to thwart this growth, the Council of Orleans (533-541) prohibited marriages between Jews and Christians and barred conversion to Judaism from Christianity. The Trulanic Synod (692) decreed that Christians could not be treated by Jewish doctors. The Synod of Gerona (1078) prohibited Christians from living in Jewish homes and forced Jews to pay taxes to support the Catholic Church. The Third Lateran Council (1179) stated that Christians could not provide certain medical care to Jews.

Pope Innocent II's Fourth Lateran Council (1215) included the following canon, which became a precedent for action by the Nazis several centuries later:

> ....(Jews) whether men or women, must in all Christian countries distinguish themselves from the rest of the population in public places by a special kind of clothing.

The purpose, according to the canon, was to prevent "criminal" sexual intercourse between Christians and Jews and making certain that "in case of such criminal intercourse, no mistake can be alleged as an excuse." It was left to the various countries to implement this decree in any manner their leaders so deemed. Two popes who succeeded Innocent (Gregory IX and Innocent IV) continued to remind followers of the need to execute the intent of the canon — which also was meant for prostitutes and lepers — and to permit no exceptions.

Authorities in England chose a design symbolizing the two stone tablets on which were inscribed the Ten Commandments. In France, St. Louis directed that the design be of a wheel and made of red felt or yellow cloth and worn both on the front and back of the clothes "so that those thus branded may be recognized from all sides." Germany adopted the rotella, a piece of yellow fabric, again in the shape of a wheel. The leaders of other countries, thinking a small badge too insignificant to accomplish the task, required Jews also to wear a hat of the same color.

So marked, the Jews then had to suffer additional pain and disgrace mandated by such ordinances as the one that accorded Christians the privilege of throwing stones at Jews on Easter. Other ordinances merely permitted the hitting or slapping of Jews at this time of year, while still others called for Jews to be pelted with mud and to run naked through the streets.

In the thirteenth century, Pope Innocent III wrote:

> The Jews' guilt of the crucifixion of Jesus consigned them to perpetual servitude, and like Cain, they are to be wanderers and fugitives...the Jews will not dare to raise their necks, bowed under the yoke of perpetual slavery, against the reverence of the Christian faith.

The Catholic Church launched a series of nine holy wars (the Crusades) from 1096-1272. The objective was to liberate the Holy Land (Palestine) from the Moslem "infidels." In the process, they murdered those they encountered who refused to be baptized immediately as Christians. An estimated one-third of Germany's Jewish population was slaughtered in the First Crusade. In Jerusalem, Jews barricaded themselves inside their synagogue to fend off the Crusaders (969 were burned to death by soldiers singing *Christ, We Adore Thee*). Thousands of Jews died in France and elsewhere. In an apparent, albeit temporary, reversal of official church position, Pope Gregory X wrote in 1272:

> We decree moreover that no Christian shall compel them (the Jews) or any one of their group to come to baptism unwillingly.
>
> .... Moreover, no Christian shall presume to seize, imprison, wound, torture, mutilate, kill or inflict violence on them; furthermore, no one shall presume, except by judicial action of the authorities of the country, to change the good customs in the land where they live for the purpose of taking their money or goods from them or from others.

In 1233, Pope Gregory IX instituted the papal Inquisition, sending Dominican friars into France and Italy. One of the goals was the conversion of Jews to Christianity. The use of extraordinarily harsh methods to elicit conversion — including torture, stiff fines, and imprisonment to gain confessions from supposed heretics — were approved by Pope Innocent IV. Those refusing to convert were burned at the stake. A similar fate befell the Jews during the fourteen-year Spanish Inquisition instigated by King Ferdinand and Queen Isabella in 1480. An estimated 30,000 Spanish Jews were burned at the stake. At the conclusion of the Spanish Inquisition, which eventually spread as far as Latin America, Jews in Spain were given the option of becoming baptized Christians or of leaving the country. Nearly 50,000 Spanish Jews died in the resulting riots. The surviving Jews, approximately 300,000 in number, were expelled from the country in 1492. Most fled to Portugal, where they were enslaved by King John II (1481-1495). They were subsequently freed by his successor but were forcibly baptized as Christians.

CHAUCER TO SHAKESPEARE

The persecution of the Jews was not restricted to the religious arena. Humiliation of the Jews also was becoming a staple of the arts. In 1380, Geoffrey Chaucer wrote in *Canterbury Tales, The Prioress's Tale* of a young Christian boy walking through a Jewish neighborhood:

> As I have said, as through the Jewry went
> This little school boy, out the song would ring,
> And joyously the notes he upward sent'
> O Alma redemptoris would he sing;
> To his heart's core it did the sweetness bring
> Of Christ's dear mother, and to her to pray,
> He could not keep from singing on his way.

> Our primal foe, the serpent Sathanas,
> Who has in Jewish heart his hornets' nest,
> Swelled arrogantly: 'O Jewish folk, alas!
> Is it to you a good thing, and the best,
> That such a boy walks here, without protest,
> In your despite and doing such offense
> Against the teachings that you reverence?
> From that time forth the Jewish folk conspired
> Out of the world this innocent to chase;
> A murderer they found, and thereto hired,
> Who in an alley had a hiding place;
> And as the child went by at sober pace,
> This cursed Jew did seize and hold him fast,
> And cut his throat, and in a pit him cast.

I say, that in a cesspool him they threw,
Wherein these Jews did empty their entrails.
O cursed folk of Herod, born anew,
How can you think your ill intent avails?
Murder will out, 'tis sure, nor ever fails,
And chiefly when G-d's honour vengeance needs.
The blood cries out upon your cursed deeds.

Throughout this confusing period, there were alternating cycles of benign acceptance of the Jews and of hatred and persecution during which Jews were corralled into ghettos and forced again to wear Judaic emblems on their clothes. There were incidents of individual violence and periodic pogroms (organized massacres of innocent people) carried out against the Jews, at times wiping out entire villages.

William Shakespeare (1564-1616) was not immune to employing in his plays characters who embodied commonly held misconceptions of the Jews. In *The Merchant of Venice* (circa 1598), Shylock, one of the main characters, is cast as a usurious Jew. In fact, Shylock is mentioned by name only three times throughout the entire play. The rest of the time he is simply referred to as the "Jew." Other times, Shylock is likened to the devil: "a kind of devil," "the devil himself," "the devil incarnal," (Act II, Scene Two). He is also likened to a dog: "be thou damned, inexecrable dog," "currish spirit governed a wolf," "for thy desires are wolvish, bloody, starved, and ravenous," (Act IV, Scene One).

The protagonist in *The Merchant of Venice*, Antonio, is a Christian who is portrayed as a charitable sort. In contrast to Shylock, Antonio is willing to lend money without interest to those in need. Shakespeare wrote that Shylock's contempt for Antonio was based on his dislike of him as a Christian in particular, and of Christianity in general.

MARTIN LUTHER

Protestant reformation architect Martin Luther (1483-1546), several years prior to nailing his famous "95 Theses" to the door of the Castle Church in Wittenberg, Germany, in 1517 to protest the selling of indulgences to raise money for the church, appeared to have much appreciation for the Jews. Early in his career, he wrote:

The Jews are blood-relations of our Lord; if it were proper to boast of flesh and blood, the Jews belong more to Christ than we. I beg, therefore, my dear Papist, if you become tired of abusing me as a heretic, that you begin to revile me as a Jew.

It soon became obvious that his magnanimous support of the Jews was predicated entirely upon their acceptance of conversion to Christianity. Such mass conversion never materialized. In 1543, Luther wrote "On the Jews and Their Lies" (a lengthy and vulgar diatribe — which, coincidentally, is longer than this book — contained in *Luther's Works*, Volume 47: *The Christian in Society IV* and translated by Martin H. Bertram) from which the following excerpts are taken:

> I had made up my mind to write no more either about the Jews or against them. But since I learned that these miserable and accursed people do not cease to lure to themselves even us, that is the Christians, I have published this little book, so that I might be found among those who opposed such poisonous activities of the Jews and who warned the Christians to be on their guard against them....
>
> What shall we Christians do with this rejected and condemned people, the Jews? Since they live among us, we dare not tolerate their conduct, now that we are aware of their lying and reviling and blaspheming. If we do, we become sharers in their lies, cursing and blasphemy. Thus we cannot extinguish the unquenchable fire of divine wrath, of which the prophets speak, nor can we convert the Jews. With prayer and the fear of G-d we must practice a sharp mercy to see whether we might save at least a few from the glowing flames. ...I shall give you my sincere advice:
>
> First, to set fire to their synagogues or schools and to bury and cover with dirt whatever will not burn, so that no man will ever again see a stone or cinder of them....
>
> Second, I advise that their houses also be razed and destroyed. For they pursue in them the same aims as in their synagogues. Instead they might be lodged under a roof or in a barn, like the Gypsies. This will bring home to them the fact that they are not masters in our country, as they boast, but that they are living in exile and in captivity, as they incessantly wail and lament about us before G-d.

Third, I advise that all their prayer books and Talmudic writings, in which such idolatry, lies, cursing, and blasphemy are taught, be taken from them.

Fourth, I advise that their rabbis be forbidden to teach henceforth on pain of loss of life and limb....

Fifth, I advise that safe conduct on the highways be abolished completely for the Jews. For they have no business in the countryside, since they are not lords, officials, tradesmen, or the like. Let them stay at home....

Sixth, I advise that usury be prohibited to them, and that all cash and treasure of silver and gold be taken from them and put aside for safekeeping....

Seventh, I recommend putting a flail, an ax, a hoe, a spade, a distaff, or a spindle into the hands of young, strong Jews and Jewesses and letting them earn their bread in the sweat of their brow.... For it is not fitting that they should let us accursed Goyim (gentiles) toil in the sweat of our faces while they, the holy people, idle away their time behind the stove, feasting and farting.... No, one should toss out these lazy rogues by the seat of their pants.

But if we are afraid that they might harm us or our wives, children, servants, cattle, etc., if they had to serve and work for us — for it is reasonable to assume that such noble lords of the world and venomous, bitter worms are not accustomed to working and would be very reluctant to humble themselves so deeply before the accursed Goyim — then let us emulate the common sense of other nations such as France, Spain, Bohemia, etc., compute with them how much their usury has extorted from us, divide, divide this amicably, but then eject them forever from the country.

I have read and heard many stories about the Jews which agree with this judgment of Christ, namely, how they have poisoned wells, made assassinations, kidnapped children.... There are many other similar stories...(and) I am well aware that they deny all of this. However, it all coincides with the judgment of Christ which declares that they are venomous, bitter, vindictive, tricky serpents, assassins, and children of the devil who sting and work harm stealthily where they cannot do it openly. For this reason, I would like to see them where there are no Christians.

Now let me commend these Jews sincerely to whomever feels the desire to shelter and feed them, to honor them, to be fleeced, robbed, plundered, defamed, vilified, and cursed by them, and to suffer every evil at their hands — these venomous serpents and devil's children, who are the most vehement enemies of Christ our Lord and of us all. And if that is not enough, let him stuff them into his mouth, or crawl into their behind and worship this holy object. Then let him boast of his mercy, then let him boast that he has strengthened the devil and his brood for further blaspheming our dear Lord and the precious blood with which we Christians are redeemed. Then he will be a perfect Christian, filled with works of mercy for which Christ will reward him on the day of judgment, together with the Jews in the eternal fire of hell!

.... My essay, I hope, will furnish a Christian...with enough material not only to defend himself against the blind, venomous Jews, but also to become the foe of the Jews' malice, lying, and cursing, and to understand not only that their belief is false but they are surely possessed by all devils.

With such high endorsement of religious prejudice, anti-Semitism was quickly becoming institutionalized. Luther's teachings, however, were not atypical of the sentiments at that time. To expel those deemed unfit was *de rigueur* policy in medieval times. In fact, Jews were driven out of England, France, Portugal, Spain, and other countries. Italian Jews were herded into ghettos and Russian Jews into a remote part of the country.

In the process, the Jews became the scapegoats of national leaders wishing to divert attention from their own shortcomings. They blamed the Jews for all ills, both perceived and real. It was not without precedent. Pope Benedict VIII in 1021 ordered the execution of Jews, believing them responsible for a hurricane and an earthquake. These were highly superstitious times, and the Jews were regularly accused of killing Christian children and using their blood in the baking of Passover bread (the Blood Libel) and also were cited as the cause of the Black Death (1348-49). In France, Spain, Switzerland, Bavaria, Rhineland, Germany, Belgium, Poland, and Austria, they were accused of poisoning wells, and tens of thousands were murdered as a result. In 1298, Jews were accused of desecrating the sacraments of Holy Communion, purportedly to recrucify Christ, causing German and Austrian citizens to massacre an estimated 100,000 Jews and obliterate 140 Jewish communities. In 1389, a priest in Prague was carrying the sacraments of communion when Jewish children playing nearby accidentally hit him with some sand. Outraged, the people killed 3,000 Jews. Inconceivable as it must have seemed, brighter days were ahead.

There were enlightened leaders who proposed that the Jews be given citizenship if they would agree to become part of the European nations in which they lived. The proposition was vigorously opposed by others, and the debate raged throughout most of the eighteenth century. The Catholic Church, however, continued to evidence its pendulous policy. In his encyclical of 1751, Pope Benedict XIV wrote:

> .... In regard to the matter of the Jews, we must express our concern... Our credible experts in Polish affairs and the citizens of Poland itself who communicated with us have informed us that the number of Jews in that country has greatly increased. In fact, some cities and towns which had been predominantly Christian are now practically devoid of Christians. The Jews have so replaced the Christians that some parishes are about to lose their ministers because their revenue has dwindled so drastically.
> .... In addition to the harm done to Christians in these regards, other unreasonable matters can result in even greater loss and danger.
> .... But if it is asked what matters, the Apostolic See forbids to Jews living in the same cities as Christians, we will say that all those activities which are now allowed in Poland are forbidden ....
> .... The essence of the difficulty, however, is that either the sanctions of the synods are forgotten or they are not put into effect. To you then, venerable brothers, passes the task of renewing those sanctions.
> ....we promise you that when the situation arises, we will cooperate energetically and effectively with those whose combined authority and power are appropriate to remove this stain of shame from Poland.

Things finally began to shift more in favor of the Jews with the American Revolution, the ratification of the Constitution, and the granting of citizenship to American Jews. Throughout much of the world, however, Jews were not prepared to move into the larger and more involved role being made available to them. As Abraham J. and Hershel Edelheit wrote in *History of the Holocaust* (Copyright © 1994 by Westview Press. Reprinted by permission of Westview Press, a member of Perseus Books, L.L.C.): "Small numbers of Jews became aware of the 'backwardness' of Jewish society and proposed remedies for all ills that kept Jews in what they saw as a cultural ghetto even while the walls of the physical ghetto were crumbling."

Emancipation of the Jews spread throughout Europe in the nineteenth century, permitting them to become involved in all aspects of society: politics, the arts, the sciences, and the aristocracy. Civil rights in exchange for adopting their country of residence were given the Jews in France (1791), Italy (1869), Great Britain (1858-1871), and Germany (1871). Still, the Jews continued to be the frequent targets of individual attacks and broader pogroms whenever current events seemed to warrant.

As the world became a more sophisticated place, the hatred of the Jews arising from medieval superstitions gradually gave way to a widespread distrust based on a paranoiac belief that Jews were somehow conspiring to take over the world.

Henry Ford

Certainly the most well-known proponent of this conspiratorial theory was none other than industrial icon Henry Ford. In the years 1920-22, Ford published a series of anti-Semitic essays in Ford's newspaper, *The Dearborn Independent.* Titled "THE INTERNATIONAL JEW: The World's Foremost Problem," the essays were later assembled in a book titled simply *The International Jew.* The pedantic and often vituperative essays purport to demonstrate a sinister international alliance of Jews. One essay, in part, reads:

> Why discuss the Jewish question? Because it is here, and because its emergence into public thought should contribute to its solution, and not to a continuance of those bad conditions which surround the Question in almost every country.... Not only does the Jewish Question touch those matters that are common knowledge, such as finance and commercial control, usurpation of political power, monopoly of necessities, and autocratic direction of the very news that the American people read; but it reaches into cultural regions and so touches the very heart of American life. The Question reaches down to South America and threatens to become an important factor in Pan-American relations. It is interwoven with much of

the menace of organized and calculated disorder which troubles the nations today. It is not of recent growth, but its roots go deep, and the long past of the Problem is counterbalanced by prophetic hopes and programs which involve a very deliberate and creative view of the future.

The essays draw heavily on the "Protocols of the Learned Elders of Zion," a document of uncertain origin. The protocols, twenty-four in all, purport to be the minutes of a late nineteenth-century meeting of Jews in which it is said, "We shall create by all the secret subterranean methods open to us and with the aid of gold, which is all in our hands, a universal economic crisis whereby we shall throw upon the street whole mobs of workers simultaneously in all the countries of Europe."

A pamphlet titled "Dialogues in Hell Between Machiavelli and Montesquieu," published in 1864 by the non-Jewish French writer Maurice Joly, appears to be the direct inspiration for the "Protocols of the Learned Elders of Zion." In the pamphlet, Joly makes no mention of the Jews whatsoever. Instead, he intended it as a satirical look at Emperor Napoleon III. The pamphlets were seized, and Joly was tried, convicted, and sentenced to French prison for his literary endeavor. The pamphlets, however, were already in circulation and began to go through a variety of transformations.

Hermann Goedsche, a German, rewrote the "Dialogues" and created a novel, titled *Biarritz*, about a sinister Jewish conspiracy. His book then was translated into Russian in 1872 and was used to support Czar Nicholas II in his fight against the nation's liberals, who supported Russian Jews. The book was once again rewritten in Paris in the late 1800s and reissued as *The Protocols of the Elders of Zion*.

The Protocols were instrumental in gathering support of pogroms in Russia, from which the number of dead will never be known. The book has undergone various revisions and editions and has been instrumental in the widespread slaughter of Jews in Russia and elsewhere. Shortly after it was distributed in London in 1920, it was exposed as a plagiaristic work based on the writings of both Joly and Goedsche. In 1921, the story of the forgery was published in a series of articles published in *The London Times* and in a book published in the same year in the United States. Still, *The Protocols* continued to be widely circulated.

Ford's *The International Jew* was translated into several languages and sold throughout the world. It remains a prominent publication, sold today primarily by white supremacist groups that apparently view the document as further proof of the international ulterior motives of the Jews.

CHARLES LINDBERGH

Even heroes can have their dark sides. A. Scott Berg, who wrote a biography of Charles Lindbergh titled *Lindbergh* (Putnam, 1998) and authorized by the Lindbergh family, reveals an anti-Semitic side of the American aviator seldom realized by the public. According to Berg, Lindbergh called Hitler a "great man" who "has done much for the German people." In an act of Nazi appreciation, Lindbergh was awarded the Service Cross of the German Eagle in 1938 from Hermann Göering.

"We are getting too many," Berg quotes Lindbergh as saying in reaction to the U.S. decision to admit Jewish emigrants fleeing Nazi Germany. Lindbergh opposed World War II, Berg says, because according to Lindbergh, it would "destroy the treasures of the White race." Lindbergh expressed a need to preserve "our inheri-tance of European blood (in) a pressing sea of Yellow, Black, and Brown."

In April 1941, speaking to 30,000 people at a meeting of the America First Committee in New York, Lindbergh said, "The British government has one last desperate plan.... To persuade us to send another American Expeditionary Force to Europe and to share with England militarily as well as financially, the fiasco of this war." Later that month, he resigned his commission as colonel in the U.S. Army Air Corps Reserve after President Roosevelt declared him a defeatist and an appeaser.

A 2000-year history of religious and racial persecution, Geoffrey Chaucer, William Shakespeare, Martin Luther, Charles Lindbergh, Henry Ford, and the *Protocols* soon were to become an unlikely alliance that would provide the political justification for the greatest horror the world has ever seen.

WORLD WAR I

With the advent of war in Europe, Jews served in the armed forces of every country involved. Nearly one-sixth of the 615,000 Jews living in Germany at the time were members of that country's military. The Jewish and non-Jewish casualties were in almost exact proportion to their respective populations. In fact, a Jew, Dr. Ludwig Haas, was the first member of the German government killed in action. He was but one of 12,000 Jews to die in German uniform.

With the realignment of boundaries following the war, many European Jews found themselves with new national allegiances. The Polish state boasted the largest Jewish population, three million. Approximately 473,000 Jews were in the new Hungarian kingdom, about the same number as in Romania. Other countries: 490,000 in Germany, 350,000 in Czechoslovakia, and 250,000 in France. The newly created League of Nations outlawed war between the countries and guaranteed the freedom and rights of all minorities.

Even after the war, the killing continued. In the Ukrainian town of Proskurov, 1,700 Jews were killed in February 1919 by followers of nationalist leader Simon Petlura. By the end of the year, they had killed at least 60,000 more Jews. Similar mass murders were occurring in Lithuania and in Poland. In Germany, however, Jews were instrumental in rebuilding the defeated country and attained positions of national leadership.

HITLER'S RISE TO POWER

In Germany, there were those who placed the blame for their country's defeat squarely on the shoulders of the Jews. Skirmishes between Jews and the anti-Semites were becoming more frequent. From this animosity arose a small political party that was eventually named the National Socialist German Workers' Party, later known simply as the Nazi party. In its twenty-five-point program published in February 1920, it called for the return of Germany's colonies lost in the war and for the creation of a nationalistic Germany. In a passage, written in part by Adolph Hitler, who had joined the party in 1919, it also stated: "None but members of the Nation may be members of the Nation. No Jew, therefore, may be a member of the Nation." It also called for the expulsion of all Jews who had arrived in Germany after 1914.

Although a minor player in the Nazi organization leadership at the time, Hitler delivered a revealing speech in a Munich beer hall in August 1920 in which he said that the Nazi party "will free you from the power of the Jew." He called for the anti-Semites of the world to unite, promising a "thorough solution...the removal of the Jews from the midst of our people."

In that same year, Hitler established the *Sturmabteilung* (SA), storm troopers who were to protect the Nazi party's meetings from violence. Because of the color of their uniforms, the SA were referred to as the Brownshirts.

His oratorical skills soon had audiences at party meetings numbering in the hundreds, and he was placed in charge of the organization's propaganda machinery. In search of an insignia to symbolize the new movement, Hitler recalled the swastikas that were used in ancient times and that adorned the Benedictine monastery he had attended as a boy. He described the eventual design (the black swastika in a white circle against a red background): "In the red we see the social idea of the movement, in the white the nationalist idea, in the swastika the mission of the struggle for the victory of Aryan man and at the same time the victory of the idea of creative work, which is eternally anti-Semitic and will always be anti-Semitic."

By 1921, leaders of the Nazi party regarded Hitler as arrogant and out of control and sought to limit his rising popularity. Hitler reacted by resigning from the party. The others, seeing in Hitler their only chance for success, begged him to reconsider. He acquiesced on the condition that he be made chairman of the party and granted dictatorial authority. The executive committee caved in to his demands. and at a July 1921 meeting, Hitler was introduced for the first time as the Führer of the Nazi Party. International events soon were to play into his hands.

The European Allies began demanding war reparations from Germany totaling $33 billion, which sowed the seeds for runaway inflation in the conquered state. The German mark soon became worthless, and hunger riots spread throughout the country. Hitler and his aides mistakenly believed it was time to strike. They mounted an unsuccessful *coup d'état* for which Hitler was convicted at a trial that brought him national publicity. He was given a light sentence and, in April 1924, was sent to Landesberg prison.

In his brief eight-month stay there, he dictated to his private secretary, Rudolph Hoess, Volume 1 of *Mein Kampf* (*My Struggle*). This book, if only the world had taken the time to read it, detailed his future plans. In it, he prioritizes people according to their physical appearance. He placed at the top of this list the Aryan man with fair complexion, blond hair, and blue eyes, describing him as the supreme human representing the master race. Hitler, invoking the words of Martin Luther from his 1543 treatise "On the Jews and Their Lies," relegated to the bottom of his perceived social order the Jews and the Slavic people. He even suggested that they would benefit from being conquered because they could learn much from the Aryans.

Hitler also mentioned Henry Ford and borrowed several phrases from Ford's "The International Jew" in *Mein Kampf*. Ford, it seems, was held in high regard by Hitler. A correspondent for *The New York Times* reported in 1922 that a large picture of Ford adorned Hitler's private office and added, "In the antechamber there is a large table covered with books, nearly all of which are a book...published by Henry Ford." Keith Sward, in *The Legend of Henry Ford* (Rinehart & Co., 1948), writes: "In the summer of 1938, the manufacturer saw fit to accept a high Nazi decoration. He received from the Chancellor (Hitler) of the Third Reich the Award of the Grand Cross of the German Eagle...the highest of all possible awards from the German state."

Released from prison in December 1924, Hitler chose to pursue his dreams through democratic rather than revolutionary means. Finding his Nazi party in shambles, Hitler organized several programs for youth, seeing in them the future hope of the Nazis. Within the brown-shirted storm troopers, he created a personal bodyguard unit he dubbed the *Schutzstaffel* (SS) and outfitted them with black uniforms.

His democratic route to power, however, was stymied temporarily by the fact that things were improving for the German people. Inflation was brought under control, and employment figures were rising. Hitler bided his time. In the 1927 elections, the Nazis fared poorly. In October 1929, the stock market crash in the United States impacted the entire world, including Germany.

In the 1930 German elections, Hitler and the Nazis mounted their most vigorous campaign to date. Hitler crisscrossed the nation delivering speeches, signing autographs, and attending torchlight parades, promising the German people jobs, prosperity, and restoration of the nation to its proper place as a world power. The Nazis won 107 seats in the German parliament, going from an insignificant organization to the second-most powerful party in the country.

The depression continued to take its toll on Germany. The government was beset by infighting and indecision, which only exacerbated the problem inside Germany. In 1932, Hitler decided to oppose incumbent Field Marshal Paul von Hindenburg for the presidency. Although unsuccessful, his national popularity continued to rise. Political chaos ensued, and violence in the streets escalated sharply. Nazi storm troopers, now 400,000 strong, roamed the cities, singing Nazi songs and instigating riots. Through protracted negotiations and coercion, Hitler was named chancellor of the German republic in January 1933.

Hitler moved quickly to solidify his position of power and forced, cajoled, and manipulated his way to the position of Führer. As undisputed dictator, he was now able to act on his hatred of the Jews.

All opposition to the Nazi party was forbidden, whether in newspapers, magazines, radio, theater, or elsewhere. The Jews, numbering only about 600,000 in a German population of six million, were officially blamed for Germany's defeat in World War I and for its economic miseries. Nazi propaganda whipped the nation's emotions into a frenzy that would support the coming sanctions against the Jews.

It is alarming to note the rapidity of the ensuing events of 1933-38 that included in sequence: a boycott of Jewish-owned businesses; a nationwide burning of books deemed counterproductive to Nazi ideals; the stripping of German citizenship from Jewish immigrants from Poland; a Nazi law —the Law for the Prevention of Progeny with Hereditary Diseases — permitting the forced sterilization of those deemed by the state to have genetic defects (*e.g.,* mental illness, retardation, physical deformity, epilepsy, blindness, deafness, and severe alcoholism); a Nazi decree forbidding Jewish ownership of land; laws barring Jews from being newspaper editors; exclusion of Jews from eligibility for health insurance; edicts prohibiting Jews from practicing as accountants, dentists, and doctors; requiring Jews to register wealth and property with the Nazi government, eventually forcing them to turn over all items of gold and silver; denying Jews the right to hold jobs in the German government; and prohibiting Jews from owning radios.

The rising storm of hatred culminated in an explosion of violence November 9-10, 1938, known as *Kristallnacht* (Night of Broken Glass). In a two-day reign of terror, an estimated 1,000 synagogues and thousands of Jewish-owned businesses and homes were destroyed. Approximately 30,000 Jewish men were arrested and sent to Dachau and other concentration camps. Many were murdered.

While the Jews were the main recipients of the Nazis' wrath, it is important to note that they were not alone. The German government enacted laws to reduce, and hopefully eliminate, those deemed to be genetically inferior to the Aryan standard. Through involuntary sterilization, several hundred African-German children and nearly 350,000 physically or mentally handicapped people were sterilized. Blacks and Gypsies* were also victims. There were other groups regarded as enemies of the state — political opponents, homosexuals, and trade unionists. Jehovah's Witnesses also were included since their beliefs prohibited them from swearing allegiance to any country or serving in the military. Jehovah's Witnesses, unlike other Nazi persecuted groups such as the Jews, could escape persecution by renouncing their religious beliefs. The majority of the 20,000 Jehovah's witnesses in Germany at the time steadfastly refused to do so and were sent to concentration camps, where an estimated 2,500 to 5,000 perished.

By 1939, more than half of the Jewish population of Germany and Austria had fled to other countries. Most went to Palestine, with others going to the United States, and elsewhere. Those who ventured only as far as Eastern and Western Europe soon came to regret their decision. Many countries — Canada, the United States, Great Britain, and France among them — strengthened their immigration laws to make it even more difficult for the German-Austrian Jews seeking asylum.

WORLD WAR II

Germany invaded Poland on September 1, 1939. World War II had begun. The Polish armies were quickly defeated, and the Nazis began massacring the country's political and social leaders, including government officials, university professors, artists, writers, Catholic priests, and others. Hundreds of thousands of Poles were relocated to make room for the "superior" German race. Thousands of others were sent to concentration camps.

Hitler then signed an order to kill those regarded as incurably handicapped. Those so designated were sent to specially constructed

---

* Gypsies came to Europe in the 1400s and were so-called because it was mistakenly thought that they came from Egypt. Comprised of "tribes" or "nations," the majority of German Gypsies were of the Sinta and Roma tribes.

gas chambers in Austria and Germany. Reacting to public protests against this practice, the Nazis temporarily abandoned the gas chamber approach, but continued the killing through lethal injection and forced starvation. The bodies were reduced to ashes in crematoria. Euphemistically called euthanasia for public relations reasons and to help insulate the murderers from the reality of their deeds, the program provided the blueprint for the Holocaust.

The German forces continued their march throughout Europe, easily conquering Denmark, Norway, the Netherlands, Belgium, Luxembourg, and France by the middle of 1941. The separation and "purification" of the defeated populations continued. In June 1941, Germany invaded the Soviet Union, followed by the mass executions of the country's political leaders, Communist Party members, Gypsies, and Jews. The killing was carried out by mobile squads (*Einsatzgruppen*). More than three million Soviet prisoners of war were murdered. Approximately 33,000, mostly Jews, were killed in the infamous massacre at Babi Yar, near Kiev.

The increasing number of prisoners from the conquered countries presented a logistical problem to the Nazis. In response, the Germans developed an intricate and vast system of concentration camps, ghettos, and forced labor camps. In Poland alone, 400 new ghettos were created to confine the Jews, tens of thousands of whom succumbed to starvation, exposure, and disease. Those consigned to the forced labor camps worked on construction projects and other hard labor, and many died from starvation, exhaustion, exposure, and physical abuse.

Beginning in August 1941, in a move perhaps inspired by Pope Innocent II's Fourth Lateran Council of 1215, all Jews were required to wear a yellow Star of David on their clothes. Other so-called "undesirables" were similarly branded. Most prisoners in the concentration camps eventually were required to wear badges of inverted triangles (*e.g.*, red for political prisoners, green for common criminals, black for Gypsies, blue for immigrants, purple for Jehovah's Witnesses, pink for homosexuals, and inverted pink triangles superimposed on yellow Stars of David for the lowest of all prisoners, the Jewish homosexuals).

At a meeting of top government officials in the Berlin suburb of Wannsee in January 1942, the Nazis agreed to implement "The Final Solution of the Jewish Question." They made a concerted effort to get rid of the ghettos by transporting their occupants to six death camps in Poland, where mass gassing machinery had been constructed, and soon began deporting Jews from all of Western Europe.

The six death camps — Chelmno, Belzec, Sobibór, Treblinka, Majdanek, and Auschwitz — were selected because of their proximity to railroad lines and because they were located in rural or semi-rural areas. All were run by the SS. Gas, as a means of mass murder, was first used at Chelmno, where it was piped into mobile vans. As many as 310,000 people were executed there during its three years of operation. Gas vans and subsequently permanent gas chambers killed up to 600,000 at Belzec, more than 225,000 at Sobibór, and perhaps as many as 900,000 at Treblinka. Majdanek and Auschwitz were both slave labor camps and death camps. An estimated 120,000 to 200,000 died at Majdanek in the gas chambers or from malnutrition, torture, exposure, and disease.

As staggering as those numbers are, the killing that took place at Auschwitz eclipses them all. The organized slaughter began at Auschwitz, located about thirty kilometers west of Kraków, Poland, with the gassing of 850 Polish and Russian prisoners, after which the science of mass executions was soon perfected. Between 1.2 to 2.5 million men, women, and children were murdered there. Nine of ten were Jews, the rest Gypsies, Russian prisoners, and others. In March 1944, the Nazis occupied Hungary. Between May 14 and July 8, more than 400,000 Hungarian Jews, including Cantor Leo Fettman and his family, were transported to Auschwitz by train in what was the single largest deportation of the Holocaust.

A total of forty-eight trains regularly converged on the six death camps from all over Europe. In nearly all instances, the men were separated from the women and children upon arrival. All were made to disrobe and to relinquish all jewelry and other items of value. Then they were told they would be given showers, which also would serve to disinfect them and rid them of lice. Forced naked, as many as 2,000 at a time, into the "showers," gas (sometimes carbon monoxide, sometimes Zyklon B, a form of hydrogen cyanide that, in diluted form, was used as an insecticide) came through the shower heads, quickly killing them all. Their bodies were stripped of hair (used for rope and for mattress stuffing) and gold and silver and disposed of in giant crematoria or in mass graves. The few who were spared the "showers" were forced to endure medical experiments, hard labor, exposure, starvation, and physical torture.

By late 1944, the Allied forces were advancing toward Germany. The Nazis abandoned many of the concentration camps and forced the surviving prisoners on "death marches" in an attempt to cover up the brutal truth of the camps. Untold thousands more died as a result.

On April 30, 1945, Hitler committed suicide in his Berlin bunker. On that same day, American forces freed 33,000 prisoners from concentration camps. On May 7, the Germans surrendered.

The immediate horror had ended. The costs, however, were incalculable. For the survivors, and for the world that could no longer ignore what had taken place, the physical and emotional recovery would never be complete.

STATISTICS

While the exact numbers will never be known, an estimated six million Jews* were killed in the Holocaust. The loss to the communities and the nations in which they lived is incalculable. In all, two out of every three European Jews had been killed. Approximately five million others, Gypsies, mentally or physically handicapped people, homosexuals, prisoners of war, resistance fighters, Jehovah's Witnesses, and other "undesirables" fell victim to the Holocaust.

Poland lost 3 million, or 90.9 percent of its pre-war Jewish population; the Soviet Union lost 1.1 million, or 36.4 percent; Hungary lost 569,999, or 69.0 percent. Other nations lost a major portion of their Jewish citizens (*e.g.*, Greece, 86.6 percent; Yugoslavia, 81.2 percent; Slovakia, 79.8 percent; and Latvia, 78.1 percent).

---

* 4,500,000 from Russia, Poland, and the Baltic; 750,000 from Hungary and Romania; 290,000 from Germany and Austria; 105,000 from The Netherlands; 90,000 from France; and 54,000 from Greece and elsewhere (Source: *1998 Information Please Almanac*).

Estimated Number of Victims in the
Major Concentration Camps

Camp	Low	High
Auschwitz	1,200,000	2,500,000
Belzec	500,000	600,000
Bergen-Belsen	35,000	50,000
Buchenwald	50,000	60,000
Dachau	30,000	35,000
Chelmno	152,000	310,000
Gross-Rosen	35,000	40,000
Janowska	30,000	40,000
Majdanek	120,000	200,000
Mauthausen	71,000	120,000
Sachsenhausen	30,000	35,000
Sajmite	47,000	54,500
Sobibór	225,000	250,000
Stutthof	65,000	85,000
Treblinka	700,000	900,000

Source: E. Kogon, Der SS-Staat, das System der deutschen Konzentrationslager, Frankfurt A/M, as cited in *History of the Holocaust,* by Abraham J. & Hershel Edelheit (Copyright © 1994 by Westview Press. Reprinted by permission of Westview Press, a member of Perseus Books, L.L.C.)

WHAT THE WORLD FAILED TO DO

Hitler's propaganda efforts and fiery rhetoric attracted much public support for his policies. The German citizens' endorsement of Nazi plans, however, was not universal. Thousands of intellectuals and artists fled the country in the years leading up to the war. Writer Thomas Mann, actress Marlene Dietrich, musician Otto Klemperer, psychologist Sigmund Freud, and physicist Albert Einstein were among them. The rest of the world remained strangely silent as the undeniable truth of Nazis' brutally oppressive tactics gradually became known.

In the 1930s, news reports of the Nazis' persecution of the Jews appeared in the United States and elsewhere. By the early 1940s, the

United States, Great Britain, and Canada were fully aware of Hitler's "Final Solution" to deport and exterminate every Jew in Europe. Still, none of these nations took official action in opposition, or even relaxed its immigration laws which would have allowed greater Jewish immigration. The major Allied powers chose instead to place the need to defeat Germany militarily over the humanitarian need to address the genocide that was known to be occurring. It was not until 1944 that public outrage pressured the government of the United States to mount efforts, albeit limited, to rescue those trapped within the concentration camps. There was one notable exception to the world's unwillingness to get involved.

The government of Denmark and its citizens succeeded on a grander scale than any other country. In September 1943, the Nazis finalized their secret plans to deport all Danish Jews. News of the impending deportation leaked out, however, and soon spread throughout the city of Copenhagen. Overnight, the country's Jews were sent word to leave their homes immediately. Hundreds of Danish citizens risked their own lives by providing the Jews with safe houses, while others formulated a daring plan to transport them by fishing boats at night to neutral Sweden. In the end, more than 7,000 Jews were saved. The Nazis captured only 700.

Church leaders, too, must share in the complicity. Although Hitler regarded all religions as roadblocks to his eventual goal of total authority over the people of Germany and the nations it conquered, the major religious authorities stood by in inexplicable silence. Paradoxically, Rudolph Hoess, who was the commandant of Auschwitz, was a devout Catholic. And at many of the death camps, the executions were suspended on Sundays so that the executioners could attend church.

The wartime leader of the Catholic Church, Pope Pius XII, continues to be criticized for his apparent unwillingness to take a stand against the actions of the Nazis. Had the Vatican simply proclaimed that the killing of the Jews was a mortal sin, it might have done much to sway the largely Christian populations of central Europe who were aiding and abetting the Nazi forces. In the absence of such a proclamation or even religious censure, Polish peasants, for example, continued to capture their country's Jews and turn them over to the Nazis in exchange for a couple of pounds of sugar.

Strong religious opposition may not have stopped the Holocaust, but it may have succeeded in minimizing the losses. Why was such opposition lacking? It is possible that Pope Pius XII felt a sense of helplessness, for the Vatican was at the complete mercy of the German troops. Perhaps, too, he feared a Nazi recrimination against Catholics. The truth may never be fully known.

On March 17, 1998, the Associated Press reported, "In a long-awaited document...the Vatican expressed remorse for the cowardice of some Christians during the Holocaust but defended the actions of the wartime pope." The Vatican's version of the Catholic Church's role during the war was contained in a report titled "We Remember: A Reflection on the Shoah" issued by the Vatican's Commission for Religious Relations with the Jews. The report had been requested by Pope John Paul II nearly a decade earlier. The Associated Press article quoted Rabbi Marvin Hier, head of the Simon Wiesenthal Center and Museum of Tolerance in Los Angeles, as saying, "To take ten years to study the critical question of the Vatican's role in the Holocaust and not to criticize Pius XII is in my view incredible. There is no denying that Pius XII did wonderful work to rescue the Jews of Rome in late 1943 and 1944, but where was he when he could have made a difference in saving the lives of six million Jews?"

Responsibility for any part of the Holocaust continues to carry a substantial price. During the war, neutral Switzerland severely restricted the immigration of Jews, yet opened wide the doors to its bank vaults accepting the confiscated Jewish wealth and the gold extracted from the mouths of Holocaust victims. In August 1998, Swiss banks settled a claim filed by Holocaust survivors by agreeing to pay them $1.2 billion for assets seized and later deposited in Switzerland during the war. There are several other lawsuits pending in which Holocaust survivors are seeking payment from several European banks, insurance companies, and manufacturers for the work they were forced to perform while in the slave labor camps.

Genocides preceded the Holocaust, and genocides have followed. Genocide (the systematic and deliberate elimination of a racial, political, religious, or cultural group) has occurred throughout recorded history. As recently as the mid-1970s, the Khmer Rouge was responsible for the deaths of two million Cambodians. Even more recently, there have been examples of genocide in the former Yugoslavia and in Rwanda. In 1998, the United Nations attempted to address the problem by issuing the draft of a treaty designed to punish those found guilty of genocide. The United States and several other world powers, however, have indicated that they will not ratify the treaty as it would mean permitting their citizens and soldiers to be tried by an international panel. The end of genocides apparently will not come about by decree.

CONCLUSION

That the Jews have survived 2,000 years of nearly relentless adversity is made even more impressive by the fact that they have indeed, during that time, continued to flourish. Given this historical background, Cantor Fettman's story offers the rest of us a glimpse as to how this has been possible. What remains most remarkable, however, is that so many of our fellow citizens of the world community persist in harboring intense prejudice and hatred based on nothing more than race or religion. The problem will not be solved by the world's political or religious leaders. Rather, the answer lies within the hearts of the people. We can all learn from Cantor Fettman's message of love and understanding. With that message, there is hope.

POSTSCRIPT

In an effort to offer a balanced historical perspective, the leaders of the Catholic Church, the Lutheran Church in America, and the Ford Motor Company were contacted and asked their views concerning the information contained in this prologue that pertained specifically to them. They also were asked what definitive steps they had taken to distance their groups from the anti-Semitic statements and actions (some centuries old, others a matter of a few decades) of their groups' predecessors, and when they took those steps. Indeed, most seem to have taken some type of remedial action, even if only within the last few years.

The Catholic Church

An inquiry to the Vatican regarding the Catholic Church's centuries-old record of abuse of the Jews was referred to the Vatican's Commission for Religious Relations with the Jews. The Reverend Remi Hoeckman (one of the three men who participated in the drafting the Vatican's 1998 report, "We Remember: A Reflection on the Shoah," referred to earlier) forwarded it to the National Conference of Catholic Bishops (NCCB) headquartered in Washington, D.C. The NCCB response:

> The key statements of the Holy See, beginning with the Second Vatican Council's NOSTRA AETATE in 1965 are included in the second edition of... *Faith without Prejudice* (Crossroad, 1993)... (including) a chapter describing the results of textbook studies of Catholic teaching materials done in 1976 and 1992 which show, in the words of Dr. Philip Cunningham (who did the 1992 study) that the ancient "teaching of contempt" to which you refer has been virtually entirely eliminated from Catholic religious education materials since the Council.

The Lutheran Church

Three synods of the Lutheran Church were contacted and asked to comment on Martin Luther's essay titled "On the Jews and Their Lies" and to describe the current position of the church regarding both Luther and the Jews.

The Missouri Synod of the Lutheran Church replied that a resolution concerning Luther and the essay was adopted at their 1983 convention and that, as a result of the inquiry, would post it on their website. That resolution reads in part:

> While The Lutheran Church-Missouri Synod holds Martin Luther in high esteem for his bold proclamation and clear articulation of the teachings of Scripture, it deeply regrets and deplores statements made by Luther which express a negative and hostile attitude toward the Jews.
> . . .Resolved, That in that light, we personally and individually adopt Luther's final attitude toward the Jewish people, as evidenced in his last sermon: "We want to treat them with Christian love and to pray for them, so that they might become converted and would receive the Lord."

The Wisconsin Lutheran Synod responded:

> Luther's attitude could be characterized as anti-Judaism rather than anti-Semitism. His opposition was not racial or ethnic but theological. ...His vehemence was directed against people who contradicted the basic truth of the gospel, rejecting the teaching that we are saved by grace alone through faith alone in Jesus as the son of G-d ....

The responses from the first two synods, while rejecting Luther's violent and hateful statements regarding the Jews, seemingly continue to embrace the religious conviction underpinning his statements (*i.e.*, that the Jews must be converted to Christianity in order to be "saved"). When asked about these responses, Cantor Fettman replied succinctly, "They can pray for my body, if they wish. But I can take care of my soul, thank you."

The Evangelical Lutheran Church in America replied that it adopted the following statement on Lutheran-Jewish relations on April 18, 1994:

> In the long history of Christianity, there exists no more tragic development than the treatment accorded the Jewish people on the part of Christian believers. ...Lutherans...feel a special burden in this regard because of certain elements in the legacy of the reformer Martin Luther and the catastrophes, including the Holocaust of the twentieth century, suffered by Jews in places where the Lutheran churches were strongly represented.
>
> .... In the spirit of that truth-telling, we who bear his name and heritage must with pain acknowledge also Luther's anti-Judaic diatribes and violent recommendations of his later writings against the Jews.
>
> ...(We) reject this violent invective, and yet more do we express our deep and abiding sorrow over its tragic effects on subsequent generations. ...we particularly deplore the appropriation of Luther's words by modern anti-Semites for the teaching of hatred toward Judaism or toward the Jewish people in our day.

Ford Motor Company

Alex Trotman, chairman of the board of Ford Motor Company, was asked about the official position of the firm regarding the infamous *The International Jew* published by Henry Ford and what the firm has done to distance itself from the anti-Semitic views embodied in the publication. He referred the inquiry to the company's corporate news department which responded:

> *The Dearborn Independent* was a personal project of Henry Ford's, not an endeavor of Ford Motor Company. ...enclosed (is) a copy of the sentiments voiced in Henry Ford's recantation of statements made in that publication, as expressed in the article from *The New York Times*, July 8, 1927.

The response from the corporate news department also included a statement that appears to come from their current personnel policies:

> Ford Motor Company maintains a strict zero-tolerance policy for harassment and discrimination.
> …The company acts aggressively on matters of harassment and discrimination in all of its facilities and takes whatever steps are necessary to ensure a workplace free from harassment of any kind.

In the 1927 newspaper article provided by Ford Motor Company, Henry Ford claims he wasn't aware of the content of the ninety anti-Semitic articles published in his newspaper, saying, "In the multitude of my activities, it has been impossible for me to devote personal attention…or to keep informed as to their contents. …Had I appreciated even the general nature, to say nothing of the details, I would have forbidden their circulation without a moment's hesitation …." Other documents provided by the Ford Motor Company, however, show that Ford's public apology was part of an effort to settle out of court a $1 million libel suit arising from one of the essays in *The Dearborn Independent*, and not the result of any remarkable change of heart. As part of the settlement, Ford also agreed to cease publication of such offensive articles and to withdraw *The International Jew* from the market. It was not possible, of course, to retrieve the copies already in circulation around the world.

Paul M. Howey

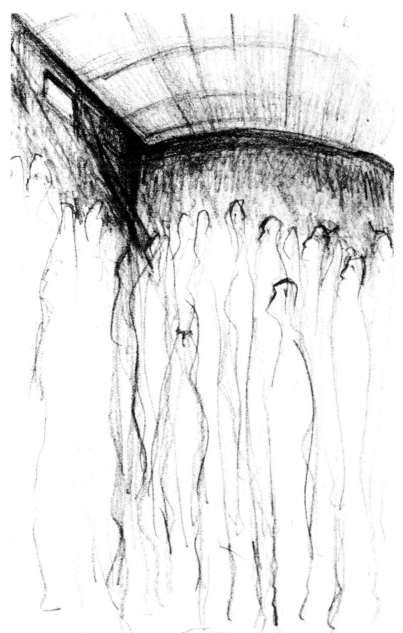

PART ONE

Chapter 1

THE SHTETL OF MY PAST

My father was filled with pride as he made his way to the synagogue Friday evening flanked by his three sons, Dezso, Sandor, and me. I remember it as a beautiful picture — my father with his trim beard, walking with his boys down the street, our side curls, called *peyes*, tossing back and forth. The earlier part of the day had been filled with preparation and much anticipation of the Sabbath.

In the Jewish faith, Sabbath begins at sunset on Friday and ends with *havdalah*, a ceremony on Saturday evening. My father always prepared the Sabbath table early in the day, carefully arranging the white tablecloth and setting out the dishes and silver candlesticks.

My mother would select a plump chicken from our backyard, instructing my older brother to take it to the ritual slaughterer. She'd spend the day with my sister, Margit, in the kitchen cooking for the Sabbath. The traditional twisted bread, called challah, had been baked in our clay oven on Thursday.

When we returned from school on Fridays, my brothers and I would sweep the floors of our little house with homemade brooms. All the rooms except the kitchen had wood floors. The kitchen floor was dirt. Then we would walk to a vacant lot about a block away from our house, where we would dig up clean yellow sand. We carried the sand home, sometimes in bushel baskets and sometimes in sacks, and we spread it carefully over the kitchen floor and over the yard. Our whole house was made so beautiful for the Sabbath!

After coming home from Friday evening prayers, my father, brothers, and I would find our home transformed into a miniature sanctuary. My mother had just lighted six Sabbath candles, one for each of us, as was our family custom. We would see Margit and my mother, both dressed in their white Sabbath dresses, sitting together at the table in the glow of the flickering flames of the candles and reading the *Tzena Urena*, a Yiddish translation of the weekly Torah portion written especially for women.

With enthusiasm, we chanted the *Shalom Aleichem*, a song meaning *Peace to You*, as we gathered at the table to welcome the Sabbath, repeating each verse three times in my father's special melody that I still use today. Turning to my mother, we honored her with the *Eishet Chayil*, a prayer in praise of the wife and mother. Next, my father blessed each child. Then everyone rose as my father, Yaakov, recited the kiddush over the wine to sanctify the Sabbath.

Each of us washed our hands before saying the *Hamotzi*. In this prayer over the bread, we bless G-d for bringing forth bread from the earth. Then my father broke the loaf apart, dipping each piece into salt before passing it to the family to enjoy. Now the special meal was served. It consisted variously of bread, gefilte fish, chicken breasts, chicken soup, and rice. We sang Hebrew songs after each course of the meal and the *Birkat Ha-mazon*, a longer prayer of thankfulness to G-d, was recited after dinner.

After dinner, the children would help my mother do the dishes. Then we would gather to share stories from the Bible and the Talmud and to sing songs. We often did not get to bed until after midnight.

From the time I was quite young, my parents taught me the historical significance and symbolism of the Sabbath dinner. During Biblical times, there were daily sacrifices of animals, birds, or crops on the Temple Mount in Jerusalem. Before the sacrifice, these were sprinkled with salt. Over the years, the Sabbath table came to represent the altar, the food and the prayers the sacrifice. The Sabbath meal is a sacred activity that carries not only this symbolism, but also the message that we should eat with civility and gratitude. Indeed, each Sabbath was, and is, a holy day.

At our dining table, each person in the family had his or her own seat. Out of respect for our parents, we never sat at their places. It was a beautiful tradition. During meals, my father used to ask us, "What did you learn today in *cheder* (Hebrew school)?" It was some kind of a test. Each of us took turns telling our parents what we had learned.

In those days, girls did not attend cheder. Instead, my sister's Hebrew school was the kitchen. Her Hebrew school was the dining room and the bedroom. Our entire home was a Hebrew school, and my mother was the teacher. I went many years to Hebrew school and to a school of higher learning called a *yeshivah*, yet my sister always knew more than I did!

I was born Eliezer Fettman on March 27, 1925, in Nyíradony, Hungary, the youngest child of Yaakov and Feige Esther Fettman. My sister, Margit, was born in 1918; my brother, Dezso, in 1921; and my brother, Sandor, in 1923.

About thirty-eight Jewish families lived in our little shtetl of Nyíradony, which was near the Romanian border. To the southwest was the big city of Debrecen. Approximately 40,000 people lived in Debrecen at the time, and it had a large Jewish community.

Most of our town's 2,000 inhabitants lived in stuccoed houses with thatched roofs and surrounded by tall, weathered fences. None of the streets in our town was paved at that time. They were all dirt roads.

My father owned a general store, which was attached to the front of our house and faced the street. In his store, he carried groceries, hardware, material to make clothing. Everything that a person needs, he had it. At night, a corrugated metal shutter was rolled down to protect the glass door to the store.

My parents' bedroom was right behind the store. Their bedroom also served as our dining room. Then came the kitchen and the children's bedroom followed one behind the other, all on one floor.

We had a shed near the house where we kept potatoes and corn. Two peach trees and two large plum trees grew in the large side yard which was about an acre in size. It was there that we kept our two dogs. We called the larger of the dogs Pengo, and the smaller one Csillag. They protected both us and the property from any intruders.

Farming was the main occupation of the inhabitants of our shtetl. Fridays were market days, when crops of corn, wheat, potatoes, barley, tobacco, fruit, and poultry were brought by cart to town.

My family also owned two small farms about seven kilometers northwest of town on the road to nearby Nyirmihalydi. One was a five-acre farm and the other about ten acres The crops were rotated between wheat and corn from year to year to help maintain the richness of the soil. My father hired two non-Jewish families to cultivate the land, and we shared the profits from the crops with them on a fifty-fifty basis. At harvest time, my mother prepared meals for the farmhands and served them in our side yard. Sometimes they requested nonkosher foods. My mother, however, could not comply with their wishes as our kitchen was strictly kosher.

My family always protected me like a baby, even as I grew older, since I was the youngest in the family. In the winter, I remember that my father always took special care to make certain that I was warmly dressed. My mother treated me much the same way, preparing my favorite foods just the way I liked them. For example, milk was always boiled before we drank it. Boiling milk, of course, creates a thin cover of scum over the surface. I didn't like the scum, so my mother always poured the milk through a strainer first. Everyone in my family was always watching out for me.

We had a wonderful home, and we always had nice clothes to wear. We had these things because my father was a very hardworking man. Although he never watched the clock, he had a set routine: morning prayers in the synagogue, back home for breakfast, and then to work in the store until the last customer of the day had left. When there were no customers, he was always studying. It was this way as long as I can remember.

Each Thursday, my father went by train to Debrecen to purchase merchandise for his store. Occasionally, I went with him and watched him go about his business dealings. Debrecen was only twenty-five kilometers away, but the train made many stops along the way, both scheduled and unscheduled. If a cow appeared on the tracks, the engineer would stop the train so he could chase it off. Sometimes the trip seemed to take hours and hours.

Twice a week, my father rode his bicycle to check on our farms. I would like to have gone with him on these trips more often; but most of the time, I was in school. I recall the time that one of the wheels of my father's bicycle hit a rock and he tumbled off, striking his head. It took him months to recover. While he recuperated, my mother ran the store, and we children helped out any way we could.

Almost every household in the shtetl owned a milk cow. The cows were rounded up in the morning and herded into the fields to graze. The streets stank of manure for hours afterwards. The owners brought their cows back in the afternoon and then milked them. Though a frail woman, my mother did the milking and made cottage cheese, buttermilk, and butter. We called our cow Piros, Hungarian for red.

A rabbi from Nagykálló once came to visit us, and my mother offered him a glass of milk. He asked if our cow had been sick. He was a very wise man, a scholar, but I have no idea what prompted him to ask this question. My mother indicated that it had. After offering a cure, the rabbi instructed us to sell the cow to a non-Jew because, under Torah law, we were forbidden to drink the milk for an extended period of time.

Summers in Nyíradony were warm but not humid and so were quite enjoyable. Winters, however, were extremely cold. The thick, thatched roof of our house provided excellent insulation. Still, in the colder months, the kitchen stove was moved into my parents' bedroom. As their room also served as a dining room on Sabbath and holidays, the cooking was done there for warmth during the winter. At night, my parents heated bricks on the stove, wrapped them in blankets, and placed them on the beds in the children's room to help keep our feet warm. One of the children's chores was to gather twigs for kindling for the stove. To start the fire a little faster, sometimes we cheated a little by sprinkling kerosene on the branches.

Of course, we had no indoor plumbing — we had an outhouse. In the winter, we ran out and back in again as fast we could. At night, we would use a little pot because, if we had to take the time to put on all our clothes, it might be too late! And we had a well. We'd turn the worn wooden crank to haul up the pail of water. The water from this well was not pure enough for drinking, so it was used only to bathe and to do the dishes and the laundry. We got our drinking and cooking water from a well about three blocks away. We had to schlep the drinking water home every single day.

Although some of the houses in our shtetl had electricity, it did not reach our home. My father begged our neighbors, both our Jewish and our non-Jewish neighbors, to help do something because we needed electricity. But there was never enough cooperation, and we never did have electricity. We had kerosene lamps — these are what we used. I remember that my father knew exactly how much fuel was required to keep the lamps lit until midnight on Friday so that nobody would have to light them during the Sabbath, which is not permitted in Orthodox Judaism.

Across from our house lived Isaac Weinberger. He was the *shochet*, the full-time ritual slaughterer. A shochet must be a pious man with a reverence for life, and his butcher's knife must be checked for nicks and honed for sharpness. Then a blessing is pronounced, and the slaughter is completed as swiftly and as painlessly as possible. Reb Isaac ("Reb" is colloquial for "rabbi" and is often used as sign of respect for another Jewish man) killed the fowl for all of us in his backyard. This was the business that he did, although he was also one of the teachers in the Hebrew school.

I don't recall that there was any industry in our town. There were farmers and professionals, but no general manufacturing to speak of. One Jew owned a printing shop down the street from our house. Another was a shoemaker, another a custom tailor. A man by the name of Markowitch was the only person on our block who did not have a business. Even today I do not know how he made a living.

Yaakov Mezei, who was a great scholar, owned a lumberyard. He studied both the Torah and the Talmud, the authoritative code of Jewish law, and he could quote a specific verse appropriate for any circumstance. Across from the Mezei family lived a wealthy Jewish couple by the name of Greenbaum, who were landowners. My uncle, Zalmen Fettman, lived with his wife, three daughters, and one son a couple of blocks away on another street. My paternal grandmother, Hitzel Fettman, lived with them. Uncle Zalmen owned a store like ours. He also raised, as I remember, white rabbits, the kind with red eyes.

❖❖❖

PIGEONS IN FLIGHT

One day, a Mr. Kende rode into town from his ranch to inquire whether or not the shochet could slaughter some pigeons. "I surely can!" Reb Isaac declared.

"Good!" exclaimed Mr. Kende. "We are celebrating a *simcha* (joyous event). I will bring them to you."

The very next week, Mr. Kende arrived with a large cage full of pigeons, perhaps fifty or more. This was simply overwhelming for Reb Isaac, so he consulted my father.

"This is more than I can handle, Reb Yaakov!" he complained. "What should I do?"

"Tell him that you must be certain that the birds can fly, otherwise they are not kosher," my father cleverly suggested.

"Most certainly, these pigeons can fly!" Mr. Kende said. With that, he opened the cage, and all the birds flew away.

❖❖❖

Next to my Uncle Zalmen lived a couple named the Hollenders. They owned a bar. The Hollenders had two daughters and two sons, one of whom, a boy named Abi, once committed some kind of crime in our little town. He may have stolen a chicken; I don't recall the specific offense.

When Abi came before the court, the judge asked, "Did you commit this crime, Abi?"

"Yes, I did," he admitted plainly.

When the judge heard that, he gave Abi a choice of paying a fine or going to jail.

"Let me go home and think about it," Abi replied. The judge allowed him to go home to decide, ordering him to return in two days. When Abi came back, he said, "I decided to go to jail, your honor."

"Why, Abi? Why don't you just pay the fine?"

"Sir, I asked my *toches* (buttocks) if they wanted to sit in jail for ten days and my toches answered, 'Yes, they would.'"

On the same street as Uncle Zalmen lived a man named Adolph Weisz. His family owned a store similar to ours. It, too, had an apartment attached to it. Rabbi Tzvi Avigdor Fish, the full-time rabbi of our little shtetl, rented this apartment from Mr. Weisz because the synagogue was nearby. Since it is tradition that we are not supposed to carry anything in public on the Sabbath, Mr. Weisz built a path for the rabbi so he could walk privately all the way to the synagogue.

Our little shtetl enjoyed everything a Jewish community might ever desire. We had a rabbi, a cheder, a yeshivah, a *dayan* (a judge in a Jewish court of law), a kosher butcher and a bakery, a shochet, and a *mikvah*. A mikvah is a ritual bath that is used by the men before each Sabbath and Jewish holiday. Women, too, would use the mikvah, immersing themselves seven days following the end of each menstrual cycle.

The synagogue, located within a large open courtyard, had two floors. The first floor was the main sanctuary, where the men would pray. On the second floor, there was a room set aside especially for the women. This room had a large window which, when open, allowed the women to hear the men's service taking place downstairs. This separation of the men and women during the services is called a *mechitza*.

The shochet, Mr. Weinberger, served as the cantor. (Cantors, as you may know, are in charge of the music in the synagogue and lead the congregation in prayer.) He was also the Torah reader and had the privilege of blowing the shofar, the ram's horn, on Rosh Hashanah. He and Rabbi Fish had beautiful voices and chanted the service with clear and resonant tones.

Mr. Weinberger's three sons also possessed wonderful voices and sang in the choir. They needed a fourth person in the choir. At the age of eight, I joined them and quickly became fascinated with singing. During the chanting of the songs, I often found myself lifted into someplace wonderful and far away.

The *shammash* is the caretaker of the synagogue. Our shammash was Mordecai Hauser, a kindly gentleman who lived in a house on the grounds of the synagogue. He acted as a *melamed* (teacher) in the Hebrew school.

A butcher shop, which was divided into two rooms, was located in another part of the courtyard. The meat was stored in one room and sold from the other.

It has long been a Jewish tradition not to cut a boy's hair before his third birthday. When I turned three, I got my first haircut To share in this celebration, many people snipped little curls from my head, and then my father gave me my first "professional" haircut.

My parents then began taking me to the cheder at the synagogue, where the rabbi taught me to read the Hebrew alphabet. To encourage me to learn, my mother baked cookies in the shape of each letter. When I recognized the letter, the rabbi put honey on the cookie, and I would eat it. Of course, before eating the cookie, I would say a *B'racha*, a blessing.

As soon as we arose in the morning, we always began the day with prayer. And we had to *daven*. Not just a little bit here and there. It was the complete davening. Davening is a light, rocking movement of the body in concert with the chanting of one's prayers. In davening, a person strives for a complete and unifying action that combines the heart, soul, and mind. In Hebrew, the process is referred to as *kavanah*, which means the concentration of prayer necessary to be able to approach the light and the power of G-d.

❖❖❖

THE "COMPLETE" DAVENING

A mother woke her son one morning. "It's time to go to school. Get up!" Still somewhat asleep, the boy came into the kitchen fifteen minutes later. "Is it time to eat yet?" he asked.

"Did you daven yet? Every morning you know you must daven when you wake up to thank G-d."

"Not yet. I only did a little davening" said the boy.

"Then, you must go back to your room and daven until you are finished!" the mother insisted.

When the son returned ten minutes later, the mother asked again, "Did you daven?"

"Yes, I did. I did enough davening and now I am ready to eat."

With a gleam in her eye, the mother went into the kitchen and brought out a plate and set it down in front of the boy. The plate had only the head and the tail of a herring lying on it. Sitting at the table, eager for his meal, the boy was dumbfounded.

"Mother, what kind of a breakfast is this? What is this lying on my plate?"

"It is a herring."

"No, it's not," the boy blurted. "It is not a complete herring. It is the head of a herring and the tail of a herring. That's what it is."

With a smile, the mother replied: "If *Ma Tovu* (the beginning of the service) and *Adon Olam* (the end of the service) are a complete service, then this fish is also a complete herring."

After breakfast, someone in my family would take me to cheder for my studies. I remained there until noon, when I walked home for lunch. After lunch, I returned to school to resume my studies until four or five in the afternoon. Then I went to the synagogue for the evening prayer. After service, I went home for dinner and then back to cheder for more lessons until 7:00 p.m. Except for the trip to school in the morning, I frequently had to walk alone and was very frightened, especially at night. From the age of three until I was six, I went to Hebrew school approximately five to six hours a day. This is what I did every day.

Not everybody in the Hebrew school had enough money to buy his own books. The rabbi had a book that we all could share. We studied at a long table, with the boys sitting along both sides. What was interesting was that the boys who sat on the right side of the table learned to read from the right. The boys who sat on the left, learned to read from the left. And the boys who faced the rabbi learned to read upside down. Many of my fellow students never learned to read correctly because of this!

When I turned six, I was required by law to attend public school eleven months out of the year. This I did from eight in the morning until I went home for lunch. Then I returned to the little ten-room schoolhouse until five in the afternoon. After supper, I — and all the other Jewish boys of our shtetl — went back to Hebrew school to study the Torah until the evening prayer service began at the synagogue.

After the service, we returned to our studies at the school, where we were paired off to learn in study groups until seven, eight, or nine o'clock in the evening. In Europe in those days, people often went to bed quite early in the evening. Many nights when I returned from school, everyone in my family was already asleep. I would walk quietly into the house so as not to wake anyone. On the stove, I always found the supper my mother had prepared for me. It's one of my fondest childhood memories.

I also recall the fragrant *cholent* that we ate at noon on the Sabbath. Cholent is a stew of beans, barley, onions, and meat or chicken — if the family could afford that luxury — plus whatever other vegetables the cook wished to include. We placed the cholent in our insulated hot oven to bake slowly all Friday night.

❖❖❖

A Cholent and the Cherry Soup

Mr. Pavel was the kosher baker in our shtetl. On Fridays, many Jews placed their cholent in his oven. As the cooking had to begin before the start of Sabbath, the oven was preheated. After the cholent was placed inside, the door was sealed with mud to insulate it while it cooked all night. Then we would pick up the cholent after the Sabbath service.

One Friday before Sabbath, Mr. Frommer, the village tailor, sent Szotak, a non-Jewish boy who worked for him, on an errand. He gave him two identical dishes, one containing cholent and the other filled with cherry soup. He told Szotak to place the cholent in Mr. Pavel's oven and to take the container of cherry soup to Mr. Engel, who owned a cold cellar.

After the service on Saturday, Mr. Frommer sent the same boy back to Mr. Pavel to pick up the cholent and then to Mr. Engel to pick up the cherry soup.

Later, when Szotak delivered the container, Mr. Frommer was already sitting at the table in great anticipation of enjoying the cholent. After saying the blessing for the family, he smiled and lifted the cover of the dish. His face flushed suddenly red. "Why is this cholent so light?" he roared. His wife stood up to peek into the bowl.

"Dried cherry seeds!" exclaimed Mr. Frommer. "The boy must have mixed up the two dishes. He probably put the cholent in the cold cellar and the cherry soup in the oven!"

❖❖❖

In my little shtetl, celebrations filled with music and prayer always signified the presence of G-d. Weddings in our community were held outside under a canopy in the courtyard of the synagogue. On Passover, the entire Jewish community came together to bake *matzah* (unleavened bread). On Chanukah, the eight-day winter festival of lights, my mother made delicious potato pancakes called latkes. On these special days, we feasted, spun a top called a dreidel, and played twenty-one, a card game.

On holidays and on the Sabbath, my mother wore a beautiful wig, called a *sheitel*. During the week, she wore a smaller sheitel called a *frizet*. She always kept her head covered, except when wearing the beautiful sheitel. It was, and still is, an Orthodox tradition that a married woman must allow herself to be attractive only to her husband. For this reason, my mother and many other Orthodox women kept their heads shaved and wore wigs.

In Central Europe at that time, every family spent the holidays on their own. It wasn't like here in America. Here, when you have Jewish holidays, it seems that the whole family goes to the grandparents' house. Over there? No. The reason for this is that my father — and every father — wanted each child to know how to celebrate the holidays. We knew how to make a Passover Seder (the celebratory meal served at home during Passover) and how to make all of the holidays. Here, everybody goes to the grandparents, and many adults don't know how to conduct a Passover Seder.

We did have guests occasionally, though usually not people from our town. Travelers, especially those people who came to see my father on business, often came to our house. And sometimes on the Sabbath, we would go to the rabbi's table to study and to socialize.

Chapter 2

SEEDS OF ANTI-SEMITISM

Perhaps the Christians in our town believed we Jews thought we were superior to them. I don't know. I do know that there was a lack of communication between us, as they were almost completely ignorant of our customs and traditions. All too often, as our world has witnessed, ignorance can breed hatred.

I must say that, before the age of six, I never knew hate resulting from the fact I was Jewish. When I began public school, I experienced for the first time the feeling that I was somehow regarded as different from others. I was often the only Jew in a class of thirty or forty students.

I found the study of Judaism to be something wonderful. The continual study of Torah gave me a feeling of closeness with G-d and a strong direction towards righteous living. *How could anyone find reasons to scorn our rituals and customs? They are so beautiful,* I thought to myself.

In public school, however, we Jewish children were often discriminated against. It really depended upon how a particular teacher felt about the Jews. During recess, some teachers did not permit us to play with the non-Jewish children. Instead, we had to stay in a separate corner of the playground. Also, if I had to go to the bathroom during the day, frequently I was not permitted. I went home many times with wet pants. As a result of all this, I grew up being very much afraid of people, even children, who were not Jewish. I despised public school but was required by law to attend. I had no choice.

Turos, a Gypsy boy with dark hair and skin, stopped me on my way to school one day. "Jew," he said menacingly, "give me money when you pass me from now on, or I will bloody your nose!" I didn't fight back. In fact, I added to this cruelty by sneaking into my father's cash drawer every morning and stealing a quarter to pay the bully.

When I went to the synagogue or to cheder, I couldn't carry my prayer books with me. Instead, I hid them under my jacket. *"Budos Zsido* (stinking Jew)!" many yelled at me in Hungarian. I always had to look around to see if there were any threatening non-Jews around. When I approached the door, I would look nervously in every direction. If the coast was clear, I would slip quickly and quietly inside.

Also, I never wore a *kipah*, also known as a yarmulke. (A kipah is the skullcap worn by Jewish men. It is worn at all times by the Orthodox, while those less observant wear them only in the synagogue.) Instead, I always wore a hat or a cap. That way, people didn't know if I was really a Jew or not. Of course, my neighbors and friends knew. But I never wore a kipah outside on the street.

This is the type of life I lived as I grew up in this small town. Anti-Semitism was all around us. It still is. You have to watch what you are saying and how you say things. It's so hard to describe. I was just an innocent child, but people pointed at me and said derisively, "Here is a Jew." I cannot adequately describe the pain I felt.

I must say that not every non-Jew in my town was an anti-Semite. We had several non-Jewish friends who were quite close, including one who gave me his birth certificate, which became very helpful to me later on. At the mere age of six, however, I knew nothing of Hungary's history nor its record of anti-Semitism. Nor did I know anything about the racist laws that the Hungarian legislature had already enacted. I knew nothing of the hatred toward Jews that was festering in Germany.

For two hours each Sunday morning, all boys were required to go to *levente*, a training center for the army. The Jewish boys were made fun of and forced to hide their long side curls under their caps. Every summer, we had off either the month of June or July from public school. During this time, we had to attend a special levente for several hours each day.

We spoke Yiddish in our home, always Yiddish. In our store, however, we only spoke Hungarian. If we spoke Yiddish, the non-Jewish customers would walk out immediately. On the street, we were not permitted to talk Yiddish, only Hungarian. Even in the synagogue, we got so used to the Hungarian language that we spoke Hungarian there, too. And this is the way it is today. Many Hungarian Jews speak only Hungarian.

In our town, anti-Semitism extended to the Christian clergy as well. The priest, for example, frequently gave anti-Semitic sermons during Easter and Christmas. "The Jews killed Christ," he would tell his congregation. "They are cursed and are representatives of Satan on this earth!" We had to board up our windows during Christian holidays because they were frequently broken.

Walking through the dark streets on my way home, I often found myself sweating with fear. Dogs might attack me. People who hated Jews might attack me. My father, sensing my nervousness, often accompanied me to and from school to help calm my fears and to protect me. Although rationally I know it has no basis, I fear dogs to this day. Even to this day, I am afraid to wear a yarmulke in public. Instead, I always cover it with a cap or a hat.

While I was painfully aware of the anti-Semitism locally, I had little knowledge of what was going on outside of our little shtetl. There was no newspaper in our community and only one radio. And this radio was owned by a Jew, a Mr. Lindenfeld. I occasionally went to his home at night to listen to it. Still, I didn't realize the magnitude of what was taking place in the rest of our country or across the world. I don't think any of the Jews in our town truly understood. If they had, perhaps some of them would have fled the country. We did hear some rumors that Jews were being taken out of their countries of Poland and Russia and being put into ghettos. But at my young age, I had no idea of what a ghetto was. Somewhere along the line, I also remember hearing the words "concentration camp"— but I didn't know what that meant either. I was to learn. Unfortunately, none of us paid enough attention at the time.

I was not even aware when the Nazis invaded neighboring Poland. And when the Hungarians, my own countrymen, began allying with the Nazis, I didn't know. There was a worldwide depression at the time, and I had no idea about this either. Maybe my parents knew of these things, but they never said a word. I had but one goal at that time and that was to study and to study and to study. That was it. I simply didn't care about the outside world.

My mother's four brothers from Hungary had emigrated to Indiana in the United States in the 1920s. Sam, David, and Sidney Weisz lived in Gary, and Ervin in Hammond. In 1938, Uncle Sam invited his mother, Hinda Weisz (my maternal grandmother), to visit, hoping that once she got there she would remain. My grandfather, Eliezer

Weisz, after whom I was named had died in 1924, and so she was alone. Shortly after arriving, she wrote us, "Everything is fine here in America, but they don't observe Judaism the way I would like them to. They don't follow the faith as closely as we do back home." Fatefully, she returned to Hungary in 1942.

The same year she came back, Uncle Sam tried again. This time he wrote an urgent letter to my father in which he said, "Get out of Hungary and come here to America! At least send Dezso." He figured that, since Dezso was the oldest, he could make the trip alone, whereas Sandor and I were still too young.

My father refused, writing back, "Sam, I have America here. Why should I go to America? I have everything I need in Nyíradony. I am well established here. It is not easy to pick up my family and move to a new country. Besides, I understand from your mother that America is not a country where you can practice our religion. The people go to America and the first thing we are told is that they throw away their *tallits*, their prayer shawls. I don't want that kind of living."

A few months later, the *dobolos* (town crier) pounded his drum as he walked up and down the streets of my little shtetl yelling, "*Kozhiretetetik, kozhiretetetik* (Hear ye, hear ye)! All Jewish men over 18 years old will be conscripted!" Under Hungarian law, young Jewish men were placed into forced labor for the government.

A day later, two *csendors* (local police) knocked loudly on our front door. "We know you have a son, Dezso, who is over eighteen years old. He must come with us!" And they took him away. I was at home when they came, and seeing my brother forcibly removed from our family was a terrible shock. I know it was even harder on my parents because he was the oldest son and they had come to rely on him to help them run the family business.

Dezso was permitted to come home two or three times during the next three years. When he returned, it was wonderful, like finding a lost child. You could see the joy in his eyes and hear the happiness in his voice to be reunited with his family. Every minute he was permitted to be with us was precious, for we never knew what would happen to him when he left. There were many stories of people who disappeared forever while in forced labor.

On his first visit home, he told us that he was an inmate at Munkaszolgalat, a labor camp located in Tasnad in northern Romania. He was working on building railroads and highways. He said he received meager amounts of food but was not paid. He described the backbreaking work, smashing rocks into gravel for the railway beds and for the roads. Although it must have been a desperate situation, he never spoke of escaping. He knew that if he didn't return to camp, our entire family would be in jeopardy.

At this time, my sister was already married with three children — two boys, Binyamin Aryeh and Zvi, and a little girl, Leah — and living in Nyírmihálydi. Margit's husband, Jakab Schwartz, owned the same type of general store as my father's.

Up until this point, few in my shtetl knew of the war in Europe or about the tyranny with which the Nazis were smothering the rights of the Jews. Only Mr. Lindenfeld, who owned a radio, had heard the news that the Nazis were rounding up Jews in Poland and in Transylvania. A few people went to Lindenfeld's house to listen to the news on the radio. My father started going there himself nearly every week. As surprising as it is, no one spoke of the news they heard for fear of upsetting others, especially the children. Also, they no doubt feared recriminations from the Hungarian government and police if they were caught spreading this news.

Early in 1942, my father and I went to Budapest to hear a speech by Rabbi Rokeach of Belz, Poland. He was a well-known rabbi, whom I remember as having a long beard and peyes. This time, however, Rabbi Rokeach appeared clean-shaven and disguised in a Hungarian military officer's uniform. His many avid followers in the Jewish underground, preparing to sneak him into Palestine, had changed his appearance so he would not look Jewish. The rabbi assured the audience that he did not think the Nazis would persecute the Jews in Hungary as they were doing in Poland. He had so much faith in G-d that he fully expected Him to intervene. Sadly — although we cannot blame him — he was gravely mistaken. Shortly after this appearance, the underground successfully spirited him away to Palestine.

Later that year, the town crier once again walked up and down the streets of Nyíradony beating his drum. He shouted, "Kozhiretetetik! Starting tomorrow, all Jews in Nyíradony must wear a yellow star on their left arm. They must also sew the Jewish star on their clothes on the left side over their heart. If this order is not obeyed, the punishment will be death!" The notice was then posted all around town.

I could see the deep sorrow in my mother's eyes as she slowly stitched the yellow emblems onto our clothes. I know it's hard to believe, but we still did not fully comprehend the threatening implications. We were just so insulated in our little shtetl. Content to retreat to the reassuring solace of our faith and the love within our families, we were slow to pay attention. Those who knew kept silent.

One day, my father called me to him after breakfast. "Leizer (as my parents called me), things seem to be getting bad. I am afraid you are the youngest one. Maybe because of the situation we are seeing, you should learn a trade and attend a nearby yeshivah to continue your Jewish studies instead of going to one farther away as we had planned." The situation for the Jews was becoming increasingly precarious, and my father wanted me to be able to come home quickly if needed. There was no yeshiva for boys over thirteen years of age in our little shtetl. The closest one was in Debrecen. Also, he wanted me to learn a trade so that I could support myself in the event that something happened to him and my mother.

Herman Frommer, who owned a tailor shop in town, agreed to teach me his craft. I learned quickly and soon learned to be a "little tailor" from him. After mastering the basics of the craft, I moved to nearby Debrecen to attend yeshiva. I was sixteen at the time. I moved in with my middle brother, Sandor, who was already living there and working as a clerk in a dry goods store. We went to the same yeshivah and I worked part time as a tailor's apprentice and continued to improve my skills. There were only two or three other people working in this little shop. The wages were barely enough to pay my rent and buy food. But the job enabled me to live and to further my religious education.

Although I'm certain our parents missed us greatly, we were in Debrecen with their blessings. Because of the size of our little town, they really had no other choice but to let us go. We did return two or three times a year, especially on Jewish holidays, unless I was involved in the synagogue choir.

My brother and I joined an Orthodox religious group for young people called Mizrachi, whose membership included about 200 young men and women. The purpose of the group was to bring the Jewish youth together for intellectual and social interaction. We studied together every Saturday afternoon. It was an active organization, and I eventually became its secretary.

As most of these students were from Debrecen, they'd had more access to world news and were quite aware of what was taking place. Several of them owned radios, and they read as many newspapers as they could get their hands on.

We came to realize that there was little future for Jews in Europe. Escape was the only choice. About a hundred of the members of our organization devised a plan for emigrating to Palestine. Sandor and I decided to join them.

Over time and with the help of our non-Jewish friends, we forged the papers necessary for such a trip. We were to leave in small groups so as not to alert the authorities, as Jewish emigration was not permitted under Hungarian law. We kept our plans secret, not even telling our parents as we knew they would not approve.

Unfortunately, someone informed the authorities of our plan, and the police began infiltrating our weekly gatherings. One Saturday afternoon, the building where we were meeting was surrounded, and we were all arrested. The authorities confiscated as many of our forged papers as they could find and threw us into jail. We were furious! But we never gave up our plans to escape the country. The story made the headlines in the Hungarian newspapers. Our parents were saddened by the news but understood the motivation behind our plan.

Luckily, I was able to keep the birth certificate given to me by Janos Szilagyi, one of my childhood Christian friends from Nyíradony. I changed almost daily the places where I hid it — buried in the ground, stashed under the eaves of the roof, in the cellar, anywhere I could think of. I even made a leather bag to protect it from the elements. It remained safe and undiscovered while I was in jail.

While in jail, members of the local Jewish community brought us kosher food. We even managed to conduct prayer services there. Eventually, we were released, but I'm certain we were under constant surveillance from that point on.

Life returned to a semblance of normalcy. I joined a choir at one of the large synagogues on Pasti street. The rabbi's name was Weisz Pal, and he was assisted by Cantor Friedlander.

Early one morning on the second day of Rosh Hashanah, a boy named Greenwald knocked on the door of the little apartment where Sandor and I lived and woke us up. Greenwald's father was a cantor at another synagogue in the city. He had run all the way to our house from the synagogue and was out of breath. "Cantor Friedlander has laryngitis and has asked that you to conduct the service at the big synagogue."

"Me? I can't do it!" I exclaimed.

"He wants to see you right away," Greenwald panted. He was trying to drag me out the door with him. Sandor jumped up from his bed. "Do it, do it!" he shouted. Together they ushered me out the door and down the street to the synagogue. The next thing I knew, I was standing in front of Cantor Friedlander in his office.

"You are going to conduct the service!" he said emphatically. It was not a question.

"But I don't know how to do it." I replied.

"But you are in the choir, and you know how to daven," Sandor countered. "Do it! Do it!"

My knees were shaking. I didn't know what to do. Besides having never led a congregation in prayer, this synagogue was different from the one in which I worshiped. Besides, what if my father found out about this? He might kill me because Cantor Friedlander led the "statesque" synagogue, the Conservative synagogue, not the Orthodox one to which we belonged.

At that time, there were three types of synagogues in Hungary. Orthodox was the most observant. The statesque could be compared to the Conservative and the neologue, the Reform. All three branches were strict in their own particular observances. All three followed the *Halakhah*, the practice of the law of the Torah. Each had its own rabbi, its own shochet, and its own dayan. Nevertheless, I felt certain my father would be upset if I were to conduct a service in the statesque synagogue. My father did much business in Debrecen, and many people there knew him. He was certain to find out. Then I had an idea.

"Cantor Friedlander," I said, "I will conduct the service on one condition. My father might not approve of my leading the service in your synagogue because he is Orthodox, so I do not want you to tell the congregants who I am."

Cantor Friedlander agreed, and I soon found myself standing before the ark. Because I was short, I had to stand on a stool. The service began with the first word "*Hamelech* (King)." Thirty voices sang the word right along with me and scared me to death. I didn't know the choir was going to sing with me. I knew the melody because I had sung it so often in the choir, so I soon became more comfortable.

"This young man asked me not to tell you who he is," Rabbi Weisz told the congregation when we finished singing. The people in the congregation couldn't see my face because I was turned away from them and facing the ark.

At the conclusion of the service and sensing that I had done quite well, I motioned to the rabbi to step closer to me and whispered, "If you want to mention who I am, you may."

Rabbi Weisz took the cue and announced to the congregation, "The young man has now given me permission to reveal his name. He is none other than Reb Yaakov Fettman's son from Nyíradony." Several gasps of surprise arose from every corner of the large synagogue.

Later, when my father learned that I had sung at the statesque synagogue, he feigned displeasure. Nevertheless, I think he was quite proud of me.

Chapter 3

THE ROUNDUP

I was putting away the Passover dishes in our small apartment when Sandor and I heard a commotion outside in the hallway. I went out to investigate. Young Jewish men and women were going door to door shouting, "The Nazis are here! The Nazis are here!" Overnight, the Nazis had entered Debrecen. The date was March 19, 1944.

There was a hastily called meeting of our Mizrachi organization. The leaders were strong in the face of this now imminent danger which we had feared for so long. They warned all of us to be vigilant and to maintain as low a profile as possible. We spoke only briefly with our friends. Most were as terrified as we were. I don't know if any of them ever succeeded in escaping to Palestine after that point, but I doubt it. It would have been almost impossible with the Nazis now occupying the city.

"Sandor, we must get home to our parents," I told my brother. He quickly agreed, and we rushed back to our apartment to begin preparing for the journey. My brother and I barely spoke. Not only were we emotionally drained, we were fearful that someone might overhear our conversations. Not wanting to schlep heavy bundles, we left all of our belongings in our apartment and packed only some food left over from Passover. Within two hours of hearing the news about the Nazi presence in Debrecen, we started for home.

Afraid to risk traveling by train, we set out on foot. We hiked across farmlands, following close to the road but not on it. We knew we had to stay out of sight of the large number of military vehicles. It was not an easy trek. It was twenty-five kilometers by highway, but we walked much farther than that, zigzagging from farm to farm along the way to avoid detection.

Twilight faded into darkness. We knew the way, but in the blackness of night, we were fearful of getting lost. Neither of us talked much. We were too terrified, exhausted, and worried about what we would find when we arrived. Every few hours, though, one of us, or sometimes both of us, would be overcome by the enormity of the situation and would sit down and weep. *What was in store for us?* I did not want to think about it. We each prayed quietly to G-d to help us.

"We can get there by morning if we keep going at this pace throughout the night," I told Sandor. He nodded in agreement and we continued.

We arrived in Nyíradony around four or five in the morning. It was still dark, and the town seemed so peaceful. Perhaps the frantic scene we'd left behind in Debrecen was just a bad nightmare. If only that were true. It was tranquil in our little shtetl only because the townspeople were asleep, still unaware of the frightening events transpiring just a short distance away.

Our parents cried tears of happiness when they opened the door to find us standing there. My father hugged us quietly for a few moments.

Once inside, my words stumbled over my brother's as we rushed to tell them everything we knew and everything we had seen. They had heard rumors that the Nazis were sweeping into Hungary, but they did not know they had already arrived in Debrecen. They were very frightened and ran around the house locking all the doors and securing all the windows. We knew it was only a matter of time before the Nazis showed up in Nyíradony.

Although she lived by herself only a few blocks away, my grandmother, Hinda Weisz, was staying in our house for Passover. We all sat together in the kitchen. No one spoke. It was impossible to put into words our feelings, our hopes, our fears. What would happen when the Nazis arrived? No one knew.

Shortly after daybreak, the townspeople began gathering in the streets. As the news spread, they began scurrying back and forth seemingly without purpose. It was as though they were bracing for a devastating flood but didn't know how to go about it. A neighbor knocked on our door, and my father opened it and stepped outside, returning just a moment later.

"The president of the synagogue told us to remain inside when the Nazis arrive," my father murmured softly. He rejoined us at the kitchen table, and the silence of fear enveloped us all once again.

Then, only a few hours after Sandor and I had arrived home, came the deluge for which our town was trying so desperately yet vainly to prepare. Hundreds upon hundreds of uniformed Nazis flooded into our little shtetl. Although our community's Jewish leaders warned us to stay in our homes, we could hear that it was total bedlam out in the streets.

The quiet inside our house was quickly shattered by screams and taunts in front of our house.

"Jews! Jews!" A large group of boys was running up and down the street with the Nazis, pointing out the houses where Jews lived. I pulled back the curtain an inch or so and watched them. I recognized many of them as having been my "friends" in public school.

The last thin veil of my childhood innocence was ripped away as two young, blond-haired men carrying machine guns and wearing Nazi armbands smashed the glass in the front door to our store and stormed into our home. Some former classmates of mine followed closely behind, smiling and snickering. We stood there speechless and frightened as the Nazis pointed their guns at us.

"This house is confiscated, *Juden*! You have ten minutes to gather your belongings and come with us!"

The taller of the two Nazis started snooping around the room. We were very angry, but we could do nothing. It was a terrible feeling of utter helplessness. They leveled their guns at us whenever we made a move or said one word. We were afraid to cough or to sneeze. Even making eye contact was a risk.

The five of us — my father, mother, grandmother, Sandor, and I —offered up prayers in silence. Three generations bound together by blood, faith, love, and now terror. We stood motionless, holding hands.

"You! Make me breakfast!" one of the Nazis suddenly commanded, pointing his finger at my father.

With a look of alarm, my father replied, "My wife will make it for you."

"Yes, I'll make breakfast for you," my mother said as she turned toward the stove.

"No, he will do it!" the Nazi commanded as he moved toward my father. My father stared for a moment at each of us. I will never forget the look on his face. Then, with a grimace, he walked stiffly toward the stove and began frying some eggs. I had never seen my father cook before. I could sense his deep humiliation and frustration at not being able to do anything to protect his family.

The Nazi devoured the eggs like a pig. He leaned back, contented with himself, and barked, "You are not coming back! Give me the keys to this house!"

My father fumbled in his pocket, pulled out the keys, and handed them to him. This young hoodlum now held the keys to our home and also our life as we knew it. How degrading for my dear father!

"We will be back in ten minutes," the Nazi repeated. "Be ready to leave! Pack your things. Each of you is permitted to have one suitcase." He clicked his heels, turned, and marched out into the street.

There was a hush of quiet. My father was the first to move. He went over to his toolbox and grabbed his hammer. He turned and stared at the sewing machine he had bought for my mother just a few weeks before. Then he began venting his fury by hitting the sewing machine over and over and over again with all of his might. He smashed it to pieces. My brother and I stood there. We froze. We couldn't move. Still no one spoke a word. We didn't know what to say.

Fighting back tears, my mother yanked the sheets off the beds. She ran to the pantry and started grabbing food and throwing it into the sheets, hastily making a package for each of us. It never occurred to me at the time, but why didn't my mother take suitcases as the Nazis told us we could? Or at least clean pillow cases? She didn't. She took the dirty sheets. My brother and I could only stand there and watch in silence. Precisely ten minutes later, the Nazis returned. They ordered us to stand outside in front of our house. Shortly, we were told, we would be taken to the synagogue.

There, in the gray morning light, I could see many Jewish families also waiting on their front stoops. I looked down the street and recognized other friends of ours walking toward us as they were being led to the synagogue. The Nazis demanded an exact spacing of twenty yards between each family, and two armed guards were assigned to each family, one behind and one at the side. They poked us with their rifles if they felt we weren't moving fast enough. The dust hung heavy in the chilly air of this spring morning as so many shoes and sandals and polished boots shuffled along our dirt streets.

Soon it was our turn to join this column of shame. We stepped into the street and began walking along behind the others. As we passed by the Weinbergers' home, I saw them waiting to leave their home forever.

Before we reached the corner, I turned to look back at our home and our garden. The young people of our town were already looting our house. I saw two of them carrying off some of our furniture. My vision was blurred by the tears filling my eyes, but I could make out our two dogs straining against the ropes that tied them to the tree in the yard. They were trying with all their strength to follow us. Helpless, all they could do was look at us with sad and questioning expressions. They had no way of understanding what was happening. Neither, for that matter, could we.

My grandmother began quietly singing the song *Zog Nit Keinmohl As Do Geist Dem Letsen Veg* (*Never Say That This Is Our Last Journey*). We all prayed privately for an immediate miracle to end all this madness. But it did not come.

"What will happen to us?" wailed one old woman. Some people were sobbing, others were stonily silent. Children were screaming. Mothers were looking up to the heavens praying to G-d for a reprieve. It was a heartrending cacophony of human despair.

For the most part, I walked in silence. I was stunned. I could not comprehend the magnitude of what was taking place or why it was happening. I felt strangely disconnected from reality. I was numb, in a state of emotional shock — I know now that I was in denial of what was taking place.

It was a tremendously sad procession as the soldiers marched us to our synagogue. "*Verfluchte Jude* (Cursed Jew)!" The Nazis cursed at us over and over while some non-Jewish children skipped alongside laughing.

When we passed by the homes of some of our close non-Jewish friends, I saw them turn their heads so they wouldn't have to look directly at us. I could see the sadness in their faces. They were as helpless as we were, and I understood that. It was, however, about the only thing I could understand.

What is going on? What is this nightmare? We pray to G-d everyday — morning, noon, and night. We thank Him and we praise Him. Does He condone what is happening to His people? Will He save us?

I tried to immerse myself in prayer as much to shut out my questions and my fears as to receive answers. The familiar walk to the synagogue seemed so strangely sinister under these circumstances. One by one, all thirty-eight families were pushed into the building by the soldiers. There were about 150 of us in all. The Nazis locked the gate of the synagogue's courtyard. Armed with machine guns and rifles with bayonets, dozens of them surrounded the area to guard us. We were prisoners in our own sanctuary.

The electric lights of the synagogue burned day and night. At first, there was a feeling of the comfort of community, crowded together as we were. Inexorably, though, fear began to seize us all once again. I prayed with all my heart for the strength to endure the trials that I sensed must lie in store for me and for my loved ones and the others. A constant murmur filled the large hall of the sanctuary. People uttered their own personal prayers again and again. They cried. They pleaded. I watched Rabbi Fish, a bearded young man in his early thirties, move through the human mass, trying to give comfort the best he could.

I sat on the floor with my family. "Father, why?" I asked him. "What will happen to us?" He did not answer, for there was no answer that he knew.

We were held hostage in our own synagogue for two long days and two very long nights. About once an hour, a black-shirted Arrow Cross, a Hungarian Nazi, strode through the sanctuary with his rifle and bayonet as a show of force.

Except for the urgent need to use the toilet, everyone remained inside the sanctuary, huddled together in fear. Parents accompanied their children to the outhouse to try to protect them from possible harm.

At night, people lay on the benches or on the floor. But everyone was too frightened to sleep. Besides, it was very cold and we had no covers. There was no firewood for the stove that normally kept the synagogue warm during the long Hungarian winters.

"Our oldest son should be with us," my mother said. "Dezso should be here. Our family should be together in this terrible crisis!" We hadn't seen Dezso for many months. We did not know for certain whether he was dead or still in the forced labor camps. I could tell my parents missed him terribly. Because he was their oldest son, they had come to rely on his strength and his love. We wanted to be with my sister, too. As I mentioned, Margit was married and living with her three children in Nyirmihalydi, seven kilometers from us. Her husband, Jakab Schwartz, was also in a forced labor camp.

In the synagogue, most of the adults talked quietly among themselves so as not to further upset the children. With prayers and reassurances, we tried to comfort the little ones and convince them that everything was going to be all right. It was not an easy task. We who were older, we who felt we should be doing something about the whole affair, were embarrassed at our inability to do anything at all. The combination of fear and helplessness drained every bit of my strength. The only thing saving me was the belief that it couldn't get any worse than this. Another day, another night spent on the floor of the synagogue.

Came the morning of the third day. We had already eaten nearly all of the food my mother had gathered in our sheet bundles. We were huddled together, staring numbly at each other when the sound of wagons broke the silence. This was followed quickly by the frightening thunder of boots as the Nazis marched quickly across the courtyard and threw open the doors of the synagogue.

"*Heraus! Heraus! Raus! Raus* (Get out! Get out! Out! Out!)" the soldiers screamed at us as they pushed us toward the door. We stumbled blinking into the bright sunshine. As my eyes became accustomed to the daylight, I saw a long line of horse-driven wagons lined up along the street in front of the synagogue. I recognized some of the wagons as belonging to our neighbors. Others were not like the low wagons our local farmers used. The side panels of these were quite high. I had never seen these wagons before.

Could they be waiting for us? I wondered to myself. There were many, many wagons. The horses clopped their hooves on the dirt road and snorted, their breath visible in the cold March morning air. They seemed anxious to get under way and to be about their task but were held in place by the reins gripped tightly in the hands of the drivers. I recognized some of the drivers as residents of Nyíradony.

When all of us were finally outside, came the order: "Into the carts, Juden!" Everyone, young and old, was shoved or thrown onto the wagons. The Nazis did not hesitate to use their rifle butts as they stuffed us like cattle onto these wagons. All of us stood, with no room to move. As soon as all of the Jewish families were loaded, the drivers' whips snapped across the backs of the horses and the wagons started moving. We had no idea where they were taking us.

As we rolled along, I peered through the slats of the wagon and could see many people lining the streets of our little shtetl, smiling, laughing at us, making fun of us, spitting on us. I recognized the faces of many of our neighbors and of my former classmates.

"*Gyu* (Move)!" the drivers cried, as our wagons rumbled slowly through Nyíradony. We rocked back and forth and bumped against one another as the wagons moved along. Then they stopped without warning, and we waited.

"The town's *bürgermeister*, Mr. Szabo, is refusing to come outside while the Nazis evacuate us," whispered Mr. Engel, who was standing behind me. "In his opinion, how the Nazis are treating us is awful!" Apparently the Nazis tired of waiting for him, and we began moving again. Soon we were in the countryside.

Everyone was too stunned to talk at first. Then the prayers and crying began again. "How can the people of the world remain silent?" I overheard one man asking no one in particular. "How can they ignore our suffering? How can they let these people do such things? Surely, they must know!"

Past farms and through villages, our string of wagons jerked and journeyed toward some undisclosed destination. Here and there, clusters of peasants gazed as we rolled by. Some just watched in silence. Others shouted curses. Because of the high sides of the wagon, I could not see them clearly; and, because of the clamor of the horses and the wooden wheels on the road, I could barely hear them. Still, I could feel their anger. It penetrated the dirt and noise like a sharp-edged knife. Over and over, I asked myself, *Why are these people so filled with hatred for us?*

Slowly we were being pulled further and further away from my little shtetl, away from my home, our sanctuary. Toward what, we were uncertain.

Would I come back someday?

After stopping for a change of horses, the wagons pushed on into and through the chill of the dark night. We arrived at the outskirts of the Hungarian town of Nyíregyháza, about forty kilometers from our home, just as dawn was breaking.

Chapter 4

Into The Ghetto

Our wagon train joined several others that were converging in a large open field. As soon as the wagons arrived, they were surrounded by armed Nazis and black-shirted Arrow Cross. We were finally permitted to get off the wagons to relieve ourselves. Of course, there was no privacy, and the whole affair was quite humiliating, especially for the women and the girls.

Within minutes, we were herded back onto the wagons. With an air of authority, the Arrow Cross began dividing the wagons, one group to the right side of the field, another to the left. Jews were being rounded up from a number of the nearby villages, assembled here, and then dispersed to two Hungarian ghettos, Varjúlapos and Nyirjespuszta. We were told that we were being taken to Nyirjespuszta.

Before I was forced back onto the wagon, I happened to spot Margit and her three children on the other side of the clearing. In her arms, she was carrying Leah, her daughter who was probably only three or four years old. I don't know if she saw us, for she was being placed back on the wagon and it was sent off in the direction of Varjúlapos. That was the last time I ever saw them.

Our line of wagons started off toward Nyirjespuszta, near a pleasant little village that lay nestled in a verdant valley. It took all day to get there. When we arrived, we found the ghetto, fully confined within a barbed-wire fence, was located just outside of town. I remember that it was a Tuesday that we arrived. The Nazis pushed us off the wagons and into barracks inside the ghetto.

They assigned us each a number that corresponded to the one that was painted on our individual bunk. The grieved look on my mother's face made my heart ache. All seemed so hopeless.

The Nazi sentries, each with a machine gun and a German shepherd, patrolled outside the ghetto. Messages blasted continuously from the loudspeakers that were positioned atop the tall barbed-wire fence — one announcement after another, one order after another. One morning shortly after our arrival came yet another.

"Attention! Attention! Young Hungarian Christians, join the Arrow Cross!" There was a pause. Then again, "Young Hungarian Christians, report to the headquarters of the Arrow Cross. Join the Arrow Cross!" This announcement was directed at the citizens of Nyirjespuszta.

My father was standing beside me at the door of our barracks. An idea flashed into my mind: *I could join the Arrow Cross! By doing so, I could help my people imprisoned in the ghetto! Did I still have the birth certificate of Janos Szilagyi? Yes, yes, here it is in my shirt pocket.*

I took a deep breath and turned to my father. "Dad, I can join the Arrow Cross. If I do, I could move in and out of this ghetto and hopefully provide some assistance for our people!" He studied the expression on my face. He knew from experience that I had a mind of my own and that, if I made up my mind to do something, I'll do it. Slowly my father nodded reluctantly and said, "Do what is necessary. But, be careful!"

"I will."

He put his hand on my arm and said, "Leizer, if you are going to act like a Nazi, we must remove that yellow star." He tore the Star of David from my jacket. "And don't you think you should look a "*bissel mehr goyish* (a little more like a gentile)?" He smiled gently, but I sensed his worry. I knew that his willingness to let me try my idea, although he gave his permission reluctantly, was an inescapable sign of how desperate he felt our situation had become.

A prayer of thankfulness came from my lips. Although the fear of uncertainty clutched at my heart, at least my family and I were still alive and relatively unharmed. I prayed, asking G-d to look with favor upon my plan.

I began studying the Nazis' routine. At all times, two guards with large dogs patrolled the perimeters of the compound. The Nazis' obsession for discipline worked in my favor. The time it took them to complete one trip around the ghetto could be timed almost to the minute. *Good! I will plan my escape accordingly.*

Although we were completely surrounded by the barbed-wire fence, we were free to move around within the compound — free to pray, free to assist those in need. Because we didn't feel any immediate danger, I don't believe that any of us could possibly have imagined what horrors the future held.

Over the centuries, the Jewish people have overcome much adversity. Therefore, I truly believed that G-d would intervene on our behalf, of that I had no doubt. The questions, however, were where and when? How long were we destined to suffer?

I began searching for some means of escape from the ghetto. I walked casually around and around the compound, discreetly examining every inch of the barbed-wire fencing. Then I noticed a small hole. Perhaps it had been burrowed by one of the many stray dogs running about. I don't know. I didn't stop to examine it. Instead, I kept walking, not wanting to draw attention to myself or my discovery.

I came across an old shed. I looked around, and when no one was looking, I slipped inside. I needed something to dig with — a trowel or shovel. In the corner, buried under a pile of rusting tools, I discovered a small spade. It was perfect. Just what I needed to widen the hole I had found, yet small enough that I could conceal it in the pocket of my trousers. I waited in that shed until the guards passed by on their rounds and then made my way back toward our barracks.

My heart was pounding as I hid behind the wall of the barracks nearest the fence and watched as the goose-stepping Nazi guards approached. Their boots pounded the dust as they marched. Even though the temperature was only in the fifties, perspiration trickled down my face and down my neck.

As soon as they passed, I ran to the hole under the fence and began digging furiously. Soon the hole was big enough, and I wriggled through to the other side. I tossed the spade in the hole and pushed dirt over the top. I had made it this far undetected, but I was not yet free.

I sprinted from one hiding place to another, where I would try to get my breath back. My heart was beating so hard now I could hear it in my ears. A bush, a tree, a shed, I used anything that would afford me cover. My eyes darted here and there. I had avoided being spotted by the advancing guards. Thank G-d, for surely I would have been shot on the spot if I had been discovered! Finally I was free for this small moment in time.

After brushing the dirt from my pants and jacket, I approached a civilian and asked where the Nazi headquarters was located. He motioned toward a building on the outskirts of town, and I walked briskly in that direction. The building appeared gray and forbidding. I hesitated for a moment on the outside steps while prayers of thankfulness and supplication swirled in my mind. I slowly opened the door.

Inside I saw two men sitting behind a long table. On the right was a Hungarian Arrow Cross official wearing a red arm band emblazoned with a black swastika, and on his left, a stern-faced Nazi.

"Present your papers!" the Arrow Cross demanded in Hungarian. "What is your name? What is your nationality? Do you have any Jewish blood?" The Nazi soldier looked me up and down. I stood at attention, trying to look as tall as possible.

"I am Janos Szilagyi, a Hungarian Christian," I said as I handed over my friend's birth certificate. "I want to join the Nazis."

"We are very careful in our selection of the men to join us," he snapped. "Tell me, Janos, why do you want to be a Nazi?"

"Because I hate Jews!"

The Arrow Cross official translated my reply into German for the Nazi, and then he turned to me. "Yes, Szilagyi. That is an excellent motive. We are recruiting Christian young men who are the true patriots of our country. Unfortunately, strange cultures have infiltrated our Hungary over the years, but we Magyars are the true heirs of this great country. If we follow Adolph Hitler's policy of racial purity and root out the budos Zsidos (stinking Jews) from every corner of this land, we will overcome their evil influence."

He studied the birth certificate carefully for several long moments before speaking. "All appears to be in order. Your hometown of Nyíradony is already *Juden rein* (Jew free). Before long, all of Hungary will be liberated from this racial pollution. Our grandchildren will be pure Hungarians. That is a genuine comfort. Just think of it! Well, Janos, your important task will be to guard these lowly dogs. You will serve your country well by doing just that for now. We both congratulate you for joining the Arrow Cross."

At that, a man approached me and handed me a black uniform and beret. The young men I had seen wearing these uniforms were cruel and vicious. It turned my stomach to assume this disguise and be associated with them. It was as if I were desecrating the very ideals

I held sacred. Yet, at the same time, I felt exhilarated by the thought that I was about to perform a mission for G-d Himself and for my people. And right under the Nazis' noses.

Through his Arrow Cross interpreter, the Nazi explained to me that my orders were to patrol the perimeter outside of the ghetto; and, if I saw a Jew outside the ghetto, I should kill him and no questions would be asked. That was my assignment.

I paused for a moment and thought about my loving family, my warm and comforting home life, and my days as a yeshivah student studying the ancient texts of the Torah and Talmud. *Why do these people despise us so deeply? Do they fear the Jewish people because they do not know us, do not understand us?* I had no answers. I did know that I was both excited and scared to death about the mission I had assumed for myself. I could be discovered at any time, even during the most common of daily routines.

We started our duties as soon as it was light out. We Arrow Cross guards were ordered to shower and shave together as a group every single morning before beginning our duties. Even this simple act could reveal to the Nazis who I really was. You need to know that I had never used a razor blade before in my entire life. As an observant Orthodox Jew, I had always used a special powder called *barbien* to remove the hair from my face, never a razor. I did my best to mimic the others and somehow succeeded without ever cutting my own throat!

Each day as I shaved, I eavesdropped on the conversations of the twenty-five or thirty other men in the bathhouse. Their talk ranged from idle chatter to the vitriolic. Much of what I heard was punctuated with anti-Semitic slurs brimming with hate and almost joyous threats of unspeakable violence. That they considered me to be one of them made me sick. Because of the course of action I had chosen, I had no other choice but to try to blend in; and so I, too, tried to speak as they did.

One morning, I heard one of the other Arrow Cross guards humming a melody that was familiar to me. I listened carefully. I couldn't identify it right away, but it began to transport me back to my days in the synagogue choir. I said to myself, *What is he whistling? Something Hebrew. A prayer maybe.*

Then it hit me! This Arrow Cross was whistling the lovely prayer *Avinu Malkenu (Our Father, Our King).*

How strange. Could he possibly be a Jew? I stuck my straightedge razor in the bar of soap and walked over to him.

"Heil Hitler!" I said to him. "My name is Janos Szilagyi. What is yours?" He gave me a name I'm certain he made up.

"What were you whistling just a minute ago?" I asked.

"Why do you ask?"

As you may know, it seems that a Jew will almost always answer a question with a question. I thought, *Aha! He's Jewish.* But I didn't say one more word to him.

The following morning, I made sure that I was standing next to him while we shaved. We talked about the Nazis and how much we hated the Jews. I looked around to see where all the others were. I waited for them to leave so I could have a private discussion with him. Finally, we were alone.

At this point, I took my bayonet, which was part of my uniform — a knife of good size — and I held the sharp edge of the blade to his throat.

"I am going to kill you because last night I found out that you are a Jew," I whispered hoarsely in his ear. Of course, I hadn't found out any such thing. I just took a chance. I figured, what did I have to lose?

"I am *not* Jewish!" he said with his voice shaking. "Take the knife away!"

"No, not until you tell me who you really are. Tell me the truth, or I will cut your throat!" I threatened.

"You are crazy! A damned Jew? No! A loyal Nazi? Yes!"

"You are a stinking Jew!" I insisted. "No Nazi would know that prayer, that melody. Admit it now, or I swear I'll kill you!"

"Let me go! I am a Nazi. I hate all Jews!"

"Listen carefully," I whispered to him. "If you admit that you are a Jew, I promise to set you free." I held the knife in my right hand and grabbed him around his chest with my other arm. I tightened my hold on him. He squeezed his eyes shut but remained quiet.

"You are right," he finally admitted. "I am a Jew! Please put your knife away," he pleaded. "I'll tell you what my name is. My name is Chaim Shlomo Engel."

When he said "Chaim Shlomo Engel," I put the knife back. "My real name is Eliezer Fettman," I told him. "How could anybody but a Jew pronounce a name like Chaim?"

Then I asked him, "Chaim, what are you doing in a Nazi uniform?"

"What are *you* doing in a Nazi uniform?" Another question answered with a question. Then he continued, "I joined the Arrow Cross to assist my people."

"I had the same idea," I said.

"When did you come into this ghetto?"

"About two or three days ago," I answered.

"You are number 19."

I couldn't figure out what he was talking about. "What do you mean I'm number nineteen?"

"Those Nazis who you just saw shaving here. Eighteen of them are Jewish. You are number nineteen."

"Really? I am number nineteen? These guards who constantly utter such hateful slander? How can I believe you?"

"We say ugly things about the Jews on purpose to dispel any suspicion about us," Chaim explained. "Besides, I've heard you say the very same things. You are certainly aware that Halakhah (Torah law) can be waived to protect a life, or in this case, thousands of lives. I tremble with fear at the thought of the horror that might befall us in the future."

I was stunned for a moment to realize that I was not the only one who had escaped the ghetto. "And what do you people do?"

"We all joined the Arrow Cross with the same idea in mind to help our people. Whenever possible, we gather secretly at night to plan ways to ease their suffering within the ghetto. We have established some trustworthy contacts there who distribute the food we bring them," Chaim explained.

"Follow me, Eliezer. I will point out some of the other Jews in our group. Remember though that spies are all around us. Be careful."

He's telling me to be careful? Was he not the one who was whistling Avinu Malkenu?

Chaim led me around the barracks secretly indicating which of the Arrow Cross were also Jews. At the same time, he would give them a sign that meant I, too, could be depended upon. It was encouraging to know that I was not alone, that plans were already under way to help our people.

We were surrounded by unthinkable hate and cruelty, yet we managed to smuggle food, water, even clothing at times into the ghetto.

We dropped these things off when no other guards or any of the ghetto Jews could see us. At the same time, we fulfilled our responsibilities as members of the Arrow Cross. We managed to communicate with one another by passing information as we walked by without ever breaking stride or even making eye contact. The possibility of being discovered by the Nazis haunted my every waking moment and more of my sleeping moments than I like to recall.

In addition to shaving, all Arrow Cross guards were required to shower together in a large communal bath. This, perhaps, was the most dangerous and most frightening part of my whole charade. Being Jewish, of course I was circumcised, and the Nazis and the true Arrow Cross were not. To identify those who were Jews, the Nazis would force those they suspected to drop their pants. I successfully escaped detection by pretending to be modest and turning away from the others to hide my circumcision. I knew I would face immediate execution, perhaps right there in the shower room, were I to be discovered as a Jew impersonating a Nazi.

I marched each day around the outside of the ghetto, carrying a rifle and guarding my fellow Jews. As I performed my duties, I looked into their pitifully sad, scared faces. They stared back at me with looks that ranged from despair to hopelessness to loathing.

The Nazis provided little in the way of food and water for those inside the ghetto. What they did give was barely enough to keep the people alive. To make certain that the people continually grew weaker, the Nazis strictly controlled the flow of traffic in and out of the ghetto to prevent extra food or water from being brought through the gates. To enforce this policy, we had strict orders to shoot on sight any Jew we saw sneaking in any provisions. If an Arrow Cross guard showed compassion to any violator, he was punished harshly.

As the days wore on, the suffering in the ghetto became more and more unbearable. Most of the ghetto prisoners had been there for several weeks. Many of them were dying of starvation and of diseases that plagued their weakened bodies. Their bloated corpses might lie in the street for days before guards loaded them on wagons and took them out of the ghetto. The pungent smell of death and decay increasingly permeated the air as the weeks wore on.

I listened helplessly to the cries coming from inside the barbed-wire fence. My own parents, grandmother, and Sandor were living in misery behind those barriers. How could I forget that? Perhaps it was they whom I heard crying.

One afternoon while I was on patrol, I noticed an old man running toward the ghetto from the town. He was a Chasid, an ultra-Orthodox Jew, with a long beard and wearing a black overcoat. I had no choice but to detain him, as other Arrow Cross guards were standing only a few yards away.

"Halt, old man!" I demanded. He stopped in his tracks. Fear showed in his eyes, and I could see him trembling as I aimed my rifle at him. "Old man, the decrees command that all Jews must remain inside the ghetto. You are violating that decree. The punishment for this, as I am certain that you know, is death."

"Please! Please don't kill me," he begged.

"Why would I kill you?"

"Because you just told me that you Nazis have orders to kill a Jew."

"That's true. I have this order," I said. But, before I kill you, let me ask you a question. How did you get out of the ghetto?"

"You wouldn't believe me."

"Try me."

"I have a wife and small children, and they are starving. When your children starve, you find a way." He pleaded with me again not to shoot him.

At this point, I was almost smiling as I looked at him. "Why would one Jew kill another Jew?"

"What are you talking about?"

"I, too, am Jewish," I told him.

"You are not. You are a Nazi!"

"I am a Jew in a Nazi uniform," I told him.

"I don't believe you."

I began to speak to him in Yiddish, and he said to me, "You really are tricky. You Nazis even learn our language."

I continued in Yiddish, "For heaven's sakes, believe me. I *am* a Jew. My parents are in the ghetto with you."

"If you are a Jew, why are you wearing a Nazi uniform?"

"So I could save your life."

As we were talking, I noticed that he appeared to have something hidden under his coat. I asked him, "What do you have there?" He showed me a loaf of bread.

"Where did you get it?"

"I stole it."

"Oh? You stole bread? Your children starve and you steal it? I understand. I want to help you, but you must do what I say. Other guards are nearby. If I make the wrong move, both of us will be killed."

The old man stood motionless. "Listen to me," I continued. "When I give you a sign, you must fall to the ground. Then I will pretend to hit you with my rifle butt. You will rise slowly and run to the gate of the ghetto."

The old man pulled his black hat down over his head but said nothing. He waited for me to make a move.

"I will try not to hurt you, but you must act like I did." I swung my rifle butt at his head and yelled, "I could kill you, you dirty Jew! Don't let me ever see you again!" A Nazi watching me looked on in disapproval.

"Run," I whispered. "Run for your life, Reb Yid!" I called him "Reb Yid," a sign of respect among male Jews, as further proof that I, too, was Jewish. He looked up at me with a dazed expression. Although he felt he could not trust my words, he had no other choice. He stood up and ran.

"Dirty, cursed Jew!" I yelled as he raced into the ghetto. I aimed my rifle over his head but decided not to fire. "Stay in the ghetto and never leave, you stinking Jew!" I shouted.

The Nazi guard approached me. I snapped to attention and said sharply, "Heil Hitler!"

"Don't you take orders from the Führer?" he demanded. "Why didn't you kill him? You have orders to kill him!"

For a moment, I really didn't know what to say. But I had always believed in G-d and I still do. I really feel that when you need G-d, G-d *is* there. So something came to my mind, and I said, "Can't you see he is an old man? Let him suffer for a few days first, then we kill him." I got away with it.

Four long weeks had passed since I had joined the Arrow Cross. The constant slander of the Jews echoed in my ears. My heart ached for my family.

Then came the announcement blaring from the loudspeakers: "Attention, Jews! Tomorrow, you will be relocated to the eastern territories, and you will not be coming back. Gather your belongings,

Jews. Relocation tomorrow. You will not be harmed. The trucks will come to take you to the train station."

My Arrow Cross comrades and I were as shocked at this news as were the prisoners in the ghetto. We had sensed that some type of relocation was in the works, but we were afraid to ask any questions for fear of drawing attention to ourselves.

Chaim approached me behind the barracks. "We will have to meet tonight," he whispered. I could hear the urgency in his voice. When we gathered later, we voted unanimously to give up our disguise and rejoin our people in the ghetto. One of the group asked, "Do any of you speak fluent Hungarian and Yiddish?" When I said that I did, they appointed me to be their spokesperson.

The next day was Tuesday. At dawn, the nineteen of us still in our Arrow Cross uniforms skipped the required showers and shaving and assembled inside the ghetto courtyard. I spoke into a bullhorn: "Attention all Jews. Come to the courtyard now!" The frightened people quickly assembled, and I ordered them to form a circle around me. We had one Jew in an Arrow Cross uniform stationed just outside the ghetto. His job was to warn us if any Nazis approached.

Then I said, "You know that you are leaving this country."

"Yes, we do," came the subdued response. One man called from the back of the crowd, "Where are you taking us? Tell us."

"We cannot divulge that information. You will find out in due time. But listen carefully. I want you to remain in this circle — all of you. We will be back in five minutes. Don't move! If we see one Jew wandering around the ghetto, we will shoot you all. Remain here!"

We all ran to our parents' barracks, removed our uniforms, and put on our regular clothes. We emerged carrying our uniforms and set them in a pile in the center of crowd of astonished Jews.

"What is going on here? This is some kind of trick!" they murmured.

"All nineteen of us are Jews!" we shouted. "We joined the Arrow Cross to help you. Now we will burn our uniforms and go with you!"

Cries came from the crowd, "It's a trick! It's a trick! They are Nazis!"

"Hold on. We are Jews! And we can prove it." I was getting desperate.

I continued, "A few weeks ago, there was an elderly Jew who left the ghetto to steal bread for his children. Will that man come forward?" The man came out of the crowd.

"I was the Arrow Cross guard who stopped you and then let you escape. Do you recognize me?"

He shook his head, "No, I do not," he said.

I did not know what to say. I looked from one Arrow Cross ally to another. All they could do was shrug their shoulders. Finally, I called out, "*Apuka* (father), where are you?" And my father came forward. "That's my dad."

Then I said, "*Anyuka* (mother), where are you?" She, too, stepped into the circle. "That's my mom." And the other boys did the same thing, and the people believed that we were Jews.

We doused the pile of uniforms with gasoline and set it ablaze. Spontaneous cheers arose from the Jews. The noise and the smoke and the flames quickly brought the Nazis. The fire department came in — two horses and a wagon. The crowd grew silent. When the Nazis saw the uniforms that were burning, they called for help. I would have to say that maybe 100 to 150 Nazis armed with machine guns and German shepherds ran into the ghetto.

"Who is responsible for this fire?" screamed the captain. "Step forward now! Step forward or every one of you will be punished!" No one moved. Silence. Once again, "Step forward or all will be punished!"

This I will never forget as long as I live. A spirit of sudden defiance gripped the captive crowd as 2,500 voices answered as one shouting, "I!" Every single Jew stepped forward at once! I stood there with tears in my eyes.

The Nazis were stunned. For once, it appeared that they didn't know what to do.

Chapter 5

RAILS TO SLAUGHTER

Shortly after dawn the next morning, April 16, 1944, every man, woman, and child was rousted from the ghetto, stuffed into waiting trucks, and driven away. The ghetto stood eerily vacant, at least for the present.

A little more than an hour later, we pulled into the Nyíregyháza train station, about forty-five kilometers from the ghetto. From the truck, I watched as steam hissed from the black engine. Behind the engine, I could see a long line of boxcars that seemed to extend to infinity.

The Nazis welcomed the unwilling travelers. "*Raus, Juden, raus!*" they shouted, pulling us out of the trucks. They shoved us onto the platform, where we stood dazed and disoriented, wondering aloud what would happen next.

"*Raus, raus!*" Loudspeakers again blared out orders, barely audible above the wailing and agonized cries. Terrified men and women; weak elderly people; teenagers and small children all were treated as though they were despised animals. Using their rifle butts to control the mob, the soldiers pushed us up the ladders into the boxcars. With the irony of hindsight, I can see that we were like a herd of cattle being led to the slaughterhouse.

Exactly seventy Jews were shoved into each boxcar. "*Eins, zwei, drei,*" until "*siebzig,*" counted the Nazis. Exactly seventy, no more, no less. I watched a small child whose parents were already on the train. This child was not permitted to follow his parents. The Nazis instead lifted him crying into the next boxcar. Seventy in a boxcar. When the allotted number was inside, the metal door was slammed shut.

The townspeople watched as the Nazi officers gloated at the frantic mass of humanity scurrying to board the train. Car after car was crammed with Jews. One after another, the steel doors slammed shut. It took hours to fill up so many boxcars. Fortunately, I was together with my father, my mother, my grandmother, and my brother. Finally, a whistle blew, and the train began to roll forward.

Was this a dream, a nightmare? Was this really happening to us? Did G-d see His people suffering? Would He redeem His people? And, if so, when?

We prayed fervently. You could hear praying amid the crying and the screaming. The boxcar was tightly packed. We stood crushed one against another with no room to move, no place to sit down, bumping into each other with each jerk of the train. Our prayers continued to flow forth.

After several hours, I found myself lapsing into an emotional lethargy. I could feel the jostling back-and-forth movement of the train, but was aware of little else. I suppose it was some kind of defense mechanism triggered by my mind. I ceased to concentrate on our situation or the people around me. I had been doing so for so long that it had drained me of all energy, even to pray. For extended periods of time, I was oblivious to the noise and confusion and despair around me and permitted myself the luxury of daydreaming about the goodness of my childhood.

In one of these prolonged moments of self-imposed isolation, I heard a voice coming from the middle of the crowd of people in our boxcar. A man was singing. His voice, his song worked their way into my consciousness. *What! Is this man crazy? We are prisoners being transported to only G-d knows where, and he is singing?*

Now I was unwillingly again in the present, forced there by a voice singing a familiar psalm, one which I had sung in the choir many times before. At first, I was irritated. But I began to get tears in my eyes as I heard another voice join in the singing, and then another. Soon there were many voices, and I added mine to this most unlikely of choirs in this most unlikely of places.

The singing had a miraculous effect on the rest of those held hostage in the boxcar — the parents stopped talking, the children stopped crying, the aged stopped moaning. The music, if only for a few brief minutes, calmed the fears and the anguish and provided us with a sense of strength through spiritual unity. When the music stopped, it was replaced only by silence as the train continued through the dark of the night.

On the morning of the second day, my father surprised me by confiding in me. "Your sister, Margit, is not your natural sibling. Before I married your mother, I was married to another woman who died. Margit was born in that marriage. I thought you should know."

I could hardly believe what he was telling me. I was hurt by the news. I had always thought she was my real sister. Then I reflected on how much I loved her. Full sister, half-sister, it didn't make any difference to me. I loved her with all my heart. And I knew from my childhood how much she loved me.

"Do Dezso and Sandor know that Margit is not our real sister?"

"Yes, they do," he admitted.

"Why didn't you tell this before?"

"You were still young. We did not think you needed to know. You have always thought of Margit as your sister. There was no reason to change that feeling," he explained.

Why was he telling me this? And why now? Is it a deathbed confession? Does he think he is going to die and he wants to bare his soul to me? Does he believe that we will never see Margit and her family again? Are we all going to die?

There were no windows, only one small, open space near the roof of the boxcar. Those who could see out through this opening would pass reports to the others. "The train is traveling through Czechoslovakia!" one man shouted.

The putrid smell of vomit, excrement, and urine stifled the air. Later, I was told that there was a bucket we could have used, but I did not see it. It made no difference as it would have been impossible to get to it, we were jammed so tightly together. There was no food, no water to sustain us, and we were growing weaker. We knew in our hearts we would not be coming back. Never again would we have the pleasant life we once enjoyed. The Nazis inflicted one terrible cruelty after another, slowly wearing us down until we almost lost the power to think as human beings. But I still could not understand. *Why were they picking on the Jews?*

The train continued to make its way down the tracks. Exhaustion overcame many of us, yet there was no room to collapse. *Can G-d read my thoughts? Can He hear my prayers emerging from this dark coffin?*

Amid the filth and wretchedness, the pain, and the suffering, I lost myself once again in thought, recalling the warmth of our family, the joy I felt at the Sabbath table, the pleasant excitement in our Yom Tov festival preparations. And I began to speak out to G-d, over and over again.

Dear Lord, through Your blessings, I have been privileged to be born into the Jewish faith, and that faith has become infused in my very being. The Torah teaches us universal ethics which should inspire all of mankind. Are we a threat to the Nazi regime that they should treat our people this way? Oh, G-d, full of compassion, You protect us and rescue us from trouble and distress, from every plague and illness. I call upon You to bring us salvation.

The train would stop every few kilometers, for water and fuel for the engine and, I suppose, to load more people. Each time, after stopping for a half hour or so, it would lurch again into the approaching night. The stinking air was nearly unbreathable. "Air, I need air. Is there any water? Please, please, some water," children moaned.

Early the next morning, the earsplitting shriek of the locomotive whistle startled us. The train was pulling into a siding somewhere. As the train slowed, we could hear many voices. And then the train stopped. *Was help on its way? Is there any hope for us?*

Suddenly, the door of the boxcar opened. A welcome rush of fresh air filled our lungs. We reached out but were quickly pushed back with rifle butts.

"Can someone help us?" mothers pleaded.

"Dirty Jews, we have water, water!" the folks at the siding shouted gleefully. "Cool water for your jewels and rings." Watches, rings, bracelets, and beads passed from hand to hand for a few precious sips of water. We had not been given any food or water when we were put on the train, so we were desperately hungry and thirsty.

The voices I heard were filled with disdain and contempt. "What good is all your gold to you now, Jew?" came a taunting cry from someone in the crowd. Indeed, water was more precious than gold.

In spite of our thirst, some of us did not barter because of the hateful slogans shouted from the townsfolk. These anti-Semites were willing partners with their Nazi comrades. Despite our weakened condition, we wanted to have nothing to do with them.

Day once again turned into night. I put my arm around my father's waist. As loving as he was, he was never very demonstrative in his displays of affection. He didn't pull away, however. Perhaps our male egos convinced us that we were embracing each other more for physical support against the swaying of the train than for emotional support. It didn't matter. It felt wonderfully reassuring. It wasn't until the first rays of the morning sunshine filtered through the slats of the boxcar that we let go of each other.

Chapter 6

ENTERING THE GATES OF HELL

We had been trapped inside this coffin on rails for two days and two nights. In some ways, it felt as though it had been an eternity. On the other hand, I was afraid for the journey to end for fear that what awaited us might even be worse, although that seemed inconceivable. It made no difference. We had lost all control of our lives as we continued to be propelled toward some unknown destination and fate.

"We are taking you to a better place." Another lie from another grinning Nazi guard who was standing outside our boxcar at one of the many stops. *Was there any reason to have hope?* They had rousted us from our homes, imprisoned us in the ghetto behind barbed-wire fences, and now they had crammed us into these miserable cattle cars.

The shrill whistle of the locomotive once again pierced the air. And again! Had we arrived at last? Were we soon to be free of this hell? I could see only desolate, treeless plains through the small opening near the roof.

Then I saw it. There was a gigantic iron gate archway bearing a sign that read *Arbeit Macht Frei* in large letters. *Work Makes Freedom.* The train passed through this gate.

The whistle screeched one last time as the train moved into a railway station to disgorge its pitiful cargo. The heat was so oppressive that it stung my eyes and made the steel surrounding us unbearably hot. I could hardly breathe. The train came to a sudden stop, one car hitting another. Once again, we were thrown into the people standing next to us, releasing renewed whimpers and wailing. Last stop! We had arrived. Where, we did not know.

From what little I could see from my vantage point, the landscape appeared gray and dead. I saw the silhouette of what looked like a factory. A large, brick smokestack belched towering black plumes into an already leaden sky. Red and yellow tongues of flames licked angrily through the top of the chimney. In the foreground were long rows of barbed-wire fencing interrupted every hundred meters or so by guard towers with large searchlights. I could make out groups of uniformed prisoners shuffling along inside the fence. They looked more dead than alive. A strange odor of decay hung in the air.

Down the line ahead of us, we could hear the boxcar doors opening and the commands of the Nazi officers as they shouted over the frantic conversations and the screams of the thousands upon thousands who were still entombed in the boxcars. My stomach churned. I tried to lose myself in prayer. *From the depths I called You. My Lord, hear my voice, may Your ears be attentive to my pleas. Give me strength to endure!*

We were alerted by the sound of the soldiers' boots as they approached. Everyone in the boxcar fell silent as the heavy door rumbled open. I was standing near the door and could see hundreds of confused, frightened people already standing on the platform alongside the train. Nazis armed with sticks and growling dogs surrounded them. A soldier with a bullhorn blared the orders: "All children and elderly must remain inside the car! Children and elderly remain inside the car! The rest may disembark. Jump out or get out now!"

As my fellow prisoners began to exit, I glanced back and saw to my horror lifeless bodies collapsing on the floor of the boxcar. About one-third of people had died during the trip. We were packed so tightly together that the dead had had no space to fall. No one knew.

The odor of the corpses swirled together with the fumes from the excrement and urine inside. The heavy air outside gave little relief as I jumped onto the platform. I looked around for my father, my mother, my grandmother, and my brother. I found them. They were all alive. Filthy, but alive. We stood shoulder to shoulder on the platform.

Then each of us was handed a postcard that read: "We have arrived safely at our destination. The Germans have treated us well. Our stay here should be pleasant and productive. Will write more later." There was a blank space for our signatures. On the threat of being shot, we were ordered to address the postcards to relatives and sign them. To whom could I send these lies? Nearly all of my immediate family members were with me. I filled in the name of a distant uncle, wrote a fictitious address, then added my signature. The postcards were collected.

Then a tall Nazi stepped up onto a small platform and looked down at us with a cold smile. His uniform was impeccable. His evil seemed impenetrable. He carried a swagger stick with which he punctuated his remarks. He spoke in German, and his words were immediately translated into several different European languages.

"My name is Dr. Josef Mengele. Welcome to Auschwitz, ladies and gentlemen." That was the time we found out that we were in Auschwitz. A shiver ran through the crowd. Some had heard of this infamous murderer and of this terrible place.

"I want the men to walk over there and form a line five people in each row," said Mengele pointing with his swagger stick. "Women over there. Five people in a row." We went to the designated places.

Once more, the Nazi with the bullhorn announced, "All children and elderly must remain on the train!" Mengele then assigned one soldier to each boxcar to remove the children. They grabbed the youngsters and babies by their arms, by their hair, by their legs, by whatever they could, and they threw them off the train like bundles of trash. Many other Nazis stood on the platform of the train station ready to catch the infants. Then they tossed some of the little ones into the air and began using them for target practice. I saw dozens and dozens of babies in the air all at one time.

I listened with horror to the staccato of the bullets from machine guns and rifles as they pierced soft tissue. Some of the SS caught the falling infants on their bayonets as part of this gruesome game. I saw a mother who recognized her child being thrown into the air, and she ran to her child. The mother and child were gunned down together. I witnessed the Nazis' delight in this game of death, which ended with the dead or mortally wounded children being thrown into a bloody pit. This is not something I saw on television or that I made up! I was there. I saw it. It is a horrible, horrible picture that is burned indelibly in my mind. I wish I could forget it; but, for many reasons that will become clear, I should not.

Next, the infirm and the extremely elderly were loaded onto Red Cross trucks. There were many, many Red Cross trucks. They filled up the trucks with these people. They drove only a short distance.

The drivers got out, climbed on top of the trucks, and dropped cannisters through openings in the roofs. They were gassing the people right in the Red Cross trucks. You could hear them screaming, but only for a moment. Then they were forever silent.

Mengele came back to where we were standing, still in rows of five. My father and brother were at my side. Mengele approached us, still smiling, and explained softly, "I am going to separate you now. I will walk among you. If I send you to the right, go to the right. If I send you to the left, go left." He stood before each of us for a split second, examining us from head to toe with his penetrating eyes. Now he pointed with his stick. "*Right, left, rechts, links, rechts, links.*" And thus was our fate determined. Every task the Nazis performed was done in a most orderly and efficient manner.

We tried to figure out what was the difference between going to the right and going to the left. As we watched, it seemed that young people under sixteen and adults over fifty or so were being sent to the left, the others to the right. Sandor and I were sent to the right. My father was sent to the left. I am certain that my mother and grandmother also were sent in that direction from the women's lines, although I couldn't see them. This was called the "selection."

I was standing next to Rabbi Fish from our shtetl. He was selected to go to the right. However, he begged the Nazis, "Can I go to the left?"

"You want to go to the left?"

"Yes."

"If you wish, certainly," Mengele grinned. "Go to the left."

Why did he want to go to the left? Perhaps, since he saw the women, the young, and the old being sent to the left, he assumed that he would not be required to do heavy labor. Our rabbi had devoted his life to prayer, Torah study, and good deeds we call *mitzvot*. He was not accustomed to manual labor. Who had any idea of the gravity of his request?

Mengele then went over to those who were sent to the left and said to them, "You must be tired after such a long journey. You are filthy. We want you to be more comfortable, so please take off your dirty clothes. You are permitted to keep your glasses, but nothing else. You will take showers to delouse yourselves and then receive clean uniforms."

Quietly and obediently, they followed his directions, arranging their clothes in neat piles at their feet. Indeed, they were dirty, and they were covered with lice. Still, I suspected this was just another way to humiliate us. A cluster of Nazis took photos and movies of them as they undressed. The Nazis were taking photographs constantly.

Once they had removed their clothes, the rumor in the camp later was that they were given small bars of soap with the initials R.J.F. (*Rein Jüdisch Fett* —Pure Jewish Fat) carved into them. There is some debate as to whether this soap actually existed. I don't know for certain. I do know that, having seen the barbaric acts of the Nazis, it would not have surprised me.

They clutched the bars of soap in their hands and began to move slowly along the cinder path toward the bathhouse. How did they know it was a bathhouse? They presumed it was because the Nazis had placed a sign that read "Baths and Disinfecting Room" in Hungarian, German, French, and Greek over the door.

At that moment, a small orchestra began playing some rather oddly cheerful music. The degradation, the brutal murders, the stench, and now the music — it was so incongruous, so surreal. I had to shake my head to make certain this was all not some terrible dream.

I watched as my parents walked through the door of the bath building. That was the last time I saw my parents.

Once they were all inside — there must have been 2,000 people crowded in there — the doors were sealed shut behind them. We soon heard the most awful sounds coming from the building. We realized then that this was a gas chamber. The people inside were crying, shouting, and singing. Yes, singing. They were singing the well known prayer *Ani Maamin* (I Believe in G-d). I turned to my brother and said, "They are murdering them, aren't they? They are murdering our people, and our people still believe in G-d?"

"Hell," I continued, "what G-d?" That was the first and last time that I ever questioned G-d. A short while later, wagons piled high with naked, lifeless bodies emerged from the building and disappeared around the corner. We had no time to absorb the magnitude of what we had just witnessed, however. Nor did we have even a moment to grieve.

Now we were also ordered to remove our clothes. We were told we had to take showers. When we entered a different shower building, we had no idea what was going to happen to us. I know it's hard to understand, but I was too numb at this point to even care. Still, there was an audible gasp of relief from this group of naked people as water did indeed come from the shower heads.

After our showers, we were approached by a group of inmates. Each one held a pair of hand clippers with which he began to do his job. They took off virtually all the hair from our heads and bodies — top to bottom. They worked in complete silence and then collected the hair into bags when they finished. We found out after the war that those inmates were also Jews and that many of them had to shave the hair off from their own parents and were not permitted to talk to them. We also were told that the hair was used for stuffing pillows and mattresses and, because of the unique reaction of hair to humidity, in the manufacture of time-delay fuses for bombs.

Then we were issued a cardboard tag on a string. Printed on the tags were our identification numbers. My number was 37276. We had to wear these tags at all times. We were not tattooed as were so many before us. I subsequently learned that the reason for this was that we Hungarian Jews had arrived at a time when the Nazis must have known that the war was turning against them. I guess they did not want to take the time to tattoo six or seven numbers on so many prisoners. They were more focused on stepping up the efficiency of their death machinery.

We were given our uniforms — blue-and-white-striped uniforms — consisting of a jacket, a pair of pants, a wraparound cap, and wooden shoes. We put them on without speaking a word. Next, we were ordered to march toward the barracks.

We passed by a fenced yard holding prisoners wearing the same striped uniforms. Their voices made us tremble, "Don't believe what they say. That factory back there is nothing more than a furnace for human bodies, Yidden. Try to save yourselves. They are going to kill you!"

Save ourselves? How? Did I dream my earlier life? Was it true? Did it really happen? If so, then what is this hell I am now experiencing? My mother and my father are dead, as well as my grandmother. All murdered. Why? Was it simply because they were Jews?

As soon as we were in our barracks, Mengele and several of his aides entered the room. "Outside, all of you!" he ordered. We gathered in front of the barracks and were lined up in rows of six.

"You over there, step forward," Mengele said quietly pointing at me. "Yes, 37276, step out. You must report to the crematorium. You will be all right." I knew by then that they lied constantly; but no matter, I had no other choice but to obey. I watched as Mengele selected several other Jewish prisoners.

"You are part of the *Sonderkommando*," one of the soldiers told us. "Now follow me." The Sonderkommando, as I was soon to learn, was a unit of prisoners assigned to work in the gas chambers and, in my case, the crematorium.

We were marched to the crematorium. It looked like a large brick oven with an arched opening. Once inside, Mengele picked another Jew and me. I'm certain he picked many others, but from where I was standing; I saw him pick only the two of us. I was ordered to stand on one side of the furnace door, and the other person from my group on the opposite side. Three Nazis stood in a row at right angles to the furnace, a few feet apart from each other. A long line of prisoners stretched across the floor of the crematorium and out the door.

These prisoners obeyed like zombies. Each was sent to the first Nazi in line, who did something to him that I could not see. Then to a second Nazi who also did something to him, but I could not see that either. By the time the prisoner reached the third Nazi, he was already more dead than alive. I could see that his chest was covered with blood. Two soldiers held the prisoner upright while a third Nazi took a small hammer and tapped out his gold fillings which fell with a clatter into a tin plate. The Nazi nodded when he finished, and the soldiers released the prisoner's arms. He fell in a crumpled heap at their feet. My partner and I were then ordered to lift the now lifeless prisoner onto a board and slide him into the furnace. Even though the heat was nearly unbearable, I stood and watched in amazement as the prisoner's skin began to blister and melt and then blacken.

My partner and I were ordered back to assist with another dead prisoner. This went on hour after hour, body after body. The longer we were there, the more I learned. I saw that the victims were given an injection of phenol in the heart before being sent to the third Nazi. The phenol caused the heart to burst, and most of the prisoners were already dead before they hit the floor.

We continued our unthinkable task, numbed by shock beyond thinking or really feeling, sliding one lifeless or nearly lifeless prisoner after another into the flames. Mercifully, after several torturous hours, an SS officer ordered us to stop. He led us into an unheated room where several other Sonderkommando prisoners sat silently. I shivered uncontrollably, although I'm certain it had as much to do with my nerves as with the cold. After the Nazi left the room, the prisoners explained that they were Polish Jews. Some were from the city of Warsaw, others from farms.

"Yidden," one whispered, "you will not stay alive for very long. You will labor for a few days in the crematorium and then you, too, will be placed in the flames. The Nazis do not want anyone to know what takes place here. One day soon, you will go to work at the crematorium and not return."

Just as soon as the prisoner finished speaking these words, the door opened and an SS officer entered. He commanded us upon punishment of death to keep secret the labor we had done that day. We were ordered to report back to the crematorium the following morning. Then two armed soldiers escorted us back to our barracks for the night.

At about 4:00 a.m. the next day, soldiers entered our barracks and ordered everyone outside for *tzel appell*, the mandatory roll call. Mengele appeared at this first tzel appell. He walked slowly past all the rows of prisoners, inspecting each of us very carefully. He moved past me, stopped, and turned around. He just stood there and stared at me. Finally, he spoke.

"Go over there," he said pointing to a spot near the fence. "You will report to work at the hospital." Last night, I was ordered to report back to the crematorium, yet now I was being told to go to the hospital? I didn't know what to do, so I quickly asked my brother who was standing next to me.

"Go over there," he whispered. "Go to the hospital."

"I can't. I have to report to the crematorium."

"You don't," my brother told me, "because Mengele did not take your number. If you go back to the crematorium, you have maybe two or three days left. If you go to the hospital, you don't know. Take a chance. Now move!"

I took a chance and never reported back to the crematorium.

After Mengele had assembled a group of about a dozen prisoners, he led us across the compound to the hospital. I soon discovered, however, that it was not a hospital at all, but rather some kind of sadistic laboratory where inhumane and utterly senseless experiments were conducted. Many of these so-called experiments resulted in crippling injuries or death for subjects. I resist telling what I saw there because many people would not believe that human beings can do such things to other human beings. But I must report that which I personally witnessed.

I was ordered to place both of my hands, palms turned up, into a large wooden vise. One of the "doctors" began turning the screws of the vise until I couldn't move my hands. Then blood was drawn from each of my fingers. He left me standing there, imprisoned in this contraption that resembled some sort of medieval torture device. He turned his back and did something with the vials of blood. When he finished, he came back and drew more blood. This scene repeated itself over and over throughout the day. I have no idea what scientific purpose this served. While the pain was severe, it was bearable. As I stood immobilized in this experimental laboratory, I witnessed unbelievable things that made my ordeal seem mild by comparison. The depravity of the Nazis seemed to know no limits.

I watched as one Nazi "doctor" injected prisoner after prisoner with air. They all died within seconds. Blood was exchanged between two other prisoners with different blood types. Neither of them survived. I watched as a prisoner was locked inside a large, glass-walled freezer. I suppose the whole purpose was to see how long he would live. The cold must have been torturous. His face permanently contorted in a silent scream, he clawed at the walls, writhing in pain before he collapsed and mercifully died. I do believe that it was because G-d was watching over me that I did survive. It could easily have been me, naked and imprisoned in that freezer, suffering that hideous and unimaginable death.

In the late afternoon, I was released from the vise and told to return to my barracks. I was weakened from the loss of so much blood — but I was alive. This time, no one ordered me to keep silent about what I had seen. Perhaps they thought no one would believe me anyway. I wasn't certain that I believed it myself, and I had seen it.

I never had to return to that hospital. In fact, my time in Auschwitz was coming to an end. It was obvious that the Nazis wanted us all dead. It did not end with the "selection" on the train platform, which divided the supposedly weak from the strong. It seemed that every day there was a "selection" process of some kind that determined who would die and who would live, at least for another day. Those whom the Nazis did not kill directly, they did away with through starvation, disease, and suicide. Those who persisted in living became prime candidates for slave labor working in the industrial trenches to keep the gears of the Third Reich's insane machinery turning.

My maternal grandparents, Hinda and Eliezer Weisz, Hungary. Eliezer died of natural causes, I was named after him. Hinda was murdered in the Shoah with my parents.

L-R: Jack, Martin, Aviva, Rachel on Leo's lap, Annette, Renana, and Miriam, 1963.

My mother and father.

Leo and Annette, Bar Mitzvah dinner, 1988.

My brother, Sandor, who perished in the concentration camp near the end of the war. How he was killed is unknown.

My sister, Margit, killed with her three children in Auschwitz.

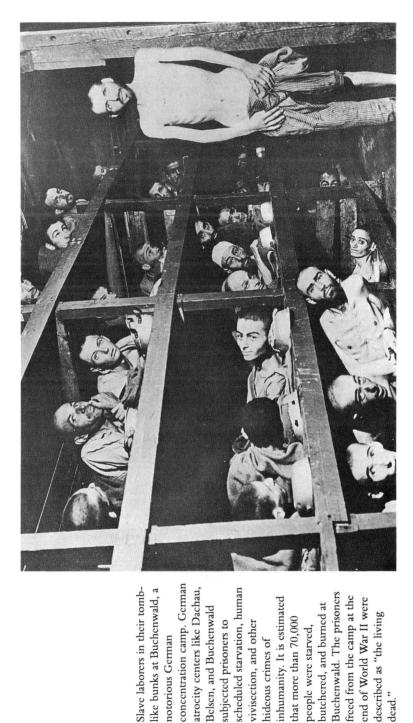

Slave laborers in their tomb-like bunks at Buchenwald, a notorious German concentration camp. German atrocity centers like Dachau, Belsen, and Buchenwald subjected prisoners to scheduled starvation, human vivisection, and other hideous crimes of inhumanity. It is estimated that more than 70,000 people were starved, butchered, and burned at Buchenwald. The prisoners freed from the camp at the end of World War II were described as "the living dead."

A mass grave at a Nazi concentration camp, 1945. At the Nuremberg war crimes trial after the war, Sir Hartley Shawcross, chief prosecutor for England, estimated that the number of people killed in the concentration camps was 12 million (this figure did not include other Nazi crimes like reprisal killings and the execution of hostages). The twelve million included 6 million Jews. Adolph Eichmann's own assessment in a report to Himmler placed the number of Jews killed at 6 million (document XPS-2615, Nuremberg). In 1944 he said: "I shall leap into my grave laughing because the feeling that I have the death of five million people on my conscience will be for me a source of 'extraordinary satisfaction.'"

Children stare at the camera shortly after the Nazi concentration camp at Petrazavodsky, USSR, was liberated by the Soviet army in 1944. The sign reads: *Entrance to the camp and conversation prohibited under threat of being machine-gunned.*

During the trial at Nuremberg in 1947, the prosecutor asked Otto Ohlendorf (commander of Einsatzgruppe D) why children were massacred: "Will you explain to the tribunal what conceivable threat to the security of the Wehrmacht a child constituted, in your judgment?" Ohlendorf answered: "According to orders, they were to be killed just like their parents. I did not have to determine the danger but the order said that all Jews including the children were considered to constitute a danger for the security of this area." He further explained: "I believe that it is very simple to explain if one starts from the fact that this order did not only try to achieve a temporary security but also a permanent security, for the children were people who would grow up and, surely being the children of parents who had been killed, would constitute a danger no smaller than that of the parents."

Belsen concentration camp.

The killing of children was a routine in the concentration camps. In the above photo, an elderly Jewish woman comforts three children as they walk to the gas chamber.

Chapter 7

SLAVE LABOR

Six days after we arrived in Auschwitz, my brother and I were assigned to Camp Wustegirsdorf, where we were sent to work for the Duebner Company. There, we were forced to grade a mountain using nothing more than very small shovels. It was backbreaking work, and if I so much as stopped to take a deep breath, a guard would hit me. All of us were black and blue with bruises at the end of every day. Wustegirsdorf was just the first of several labor camps to which we would be assigned. We were constantly being moved from one camp to another.

The physical layout of the various labor camps, however, was quite similar. Every camp had approximately twenty wooden barracks, each housing twenty prisoners. There was a round bench in the center of the barracks where we sat while we ate. There were no beds, so we had to sleep on the floor in our uniforms. It was very crowded. If somebody was uncomfortable during the night and wanted to turn over, we all had to turn in the same direction on the count of three. Everyone had to sleep on the same side. Odd as it sounds, this provided us with a bit of comic relief.

We were always looking for something humorous to distract us from our miserable existence. One evening, while we rested after a day's labor, a prisoner ran by yelling, "Oy, what I saw was terrible."

"What did you see?" someone asked.

"I saw a dead dog!" he exclaimed.

"What! Is this good for the Jews?"

Yes, strange as it sounds, we found that quite funny! Without some humor, no one could have survived these camps.

The latrines were usually in another building, although in some camps they were out in the open. The latrines were simply long pits with heavy rods set along the length of them on which one sat. One had to be very careful not to fall in.

Just as in Auschwitz, the Nazi guards woke us before dawn every morning. We had to report immediately to the center of the campground for tzel appell. The Nazis counted us as we stood at attention, five prisoners in a row. We were required to stand motionless for one hour every morning. You were not permitted even to move your fingers or turn your head. You had to stand ramrod straight, for at least sixty minutes every morning. If the prisoner count matched the guards' records, the tzel appell could be over within one hour. Some tzel appells lasted as long as six.

Many people were not able to stand still that long. The Nazis, with their machine guns and their snarling German shepherds, would walk up and down the rows of prisoners. If a prisoner made the slightest move, he was shot on the spot. There were those who did not want to live. They wanted to die. So they moved, and they were killed.

While we were standing there, the guards would go to our barracks and count the prisoners who had died during the night. The prisoner count always had to match the guards' records. It didn't matter whether the prisoner was dead or alive, just that his number was counted. When tzel appell finally ended, we returned to the barracks and loaded onto a wagon the bodies of those who had died during the night. The local townsfolk then picked up the bodies for burial outside the camp.

The tzel appell was a daily ritual regardless of the weather conditions. How we managed to survive the freezing winds and rain and snow, wearing pajama-like uniforms, no underwear, no socks, I do not know. Many, sadly, did not.

Breakfast, such as it was, followed the tzel appell. Food? We didn't really know what food was. I will tell you, however, what I ate for the thirteen months I was in these camps. Every single morning, the Nazis prepared a large kettle of coffee for themselves. After they drank the coffee, they stirred cold water into the grounds remaining in the bottom of the pot and served it to us. That was our breakfast. Cold, black water. Lunchtime, the same thing. Still, we stood anxiously in line with our tin bowls at each "meal" because we knew that we had to eat something. I had to hold my bowl tightly because the Nazis threw the "food" at our bowls. If you dropped your portion, that would be that.

For dinner, it was entirely different. The farmers used to bring potatoes into the camp for the soldiers. The Nazis filled up a big pot with water and placed the potatoes in it to wash them. They took the potatoes for themselves, and we had the dirty water. If we were lucky, we would find a few potato peelings here and there.

Every night before we went to sleep, they would give us a loaf of bread. One small loaf for twenty starving people. A loaf of bread and a piece of string. Each night, a different person would be assigned to cut the bread with the string as well as he could and then distribute each precious slice. There was always a big argument about how thin or thick the slices were cut.

I will never forget the first time that they gave us the bread. A few of us went to wash our hands before eating the bread, as was our custom. We returned to discover that our portions had been stolen. Brother would steal from brother, so great was our hunger. After that first sad lesson, everyone ate his bread at once. We never left a crumb.

Every day, we had to walk about five kilometers to work. The German townsfolk would stare at us in silence. One evening, however, as we were coming back to camp from work, some "angel" threw potatoes and bread to us in the darkness.

In camp, I frequently had reason to recall the Jewish parable:

> A man was escorted to a place that had several rooms but was not told if any of the rooms were heaven or hell. The rooms were all the same. People were standing on both sides of tables, which were loaded with food. But their bodies were stiff, they could neither bend at the waist nor could they bend their arms at the elbows. Therefore, the people had no way to feed themselves. After passing each of the rooms, the man suspected that they might all be hell despite the abundance of food.
>
> Then he went back into one room and noticed that a change had occurred. The people's bodies were still stiff, but they were grasping the food with their hands, extending their stiffened arms, and feeding the people directly across the table from them.
>
> The man knew then that the room was heaven.

I had no doubt that I was not yet in heaven.

After Wustegirsdorf, Sandor and I were assigned to the Wustewaltersdorf labor camp, where we worked for the Jank Company doing highway construction. Our job was to move gravel in small wheelbarrows from one location to another, about fifty meters apart, twelve hours a day, every day of the week. All construction work was done manually. In all the camps, I never saw a machine that the prisoners were permitted to use.

I also worked for another company while in this camp. While I can't remember the name of the company, it is impossible for me to forget the labor that we did. We worked in railroad construction. Two of us had to carry railroad ties and set them in place. Then we would turn around and carry a long, heavy iron rail and place it on the ties. Several of the starving inmates collapsed under the weight. Those who did were shot.

The second day in Wustewaltersdorf, we got to know Oscar, the camp's *Kapo* (Lagerältestes, also known as Kapos, were senior camp prisoners who were given special privileges in exchange for supervising other prisoners.) Many of the Kapos I encountered were more brutal than the Nazi guards. I suppose this is why they were chosen for this job. A few Kapos, like Oscar for example, were more considerate.

One day, Oscar told us that he had a pair of *tefillin* that had been smuggled into camp. This had much importance to us. According to the books of Exodus and Deuteronomy, Jews must bind the commandments upon their hands and between their eyes. This is done by placing the Biblical passages in special boxes called tefillin, which are then tied with leather straps over the forehead and around the arm. It is to be done each weekday by Jewish men. To have tefillin, if even briefly, allowed us to reconnect to our faith in a very meaningful way.

Oscar said that if we wanted to don the tefillin for a few seconds, we could do so. Every day while I was in this camp, I put on the tefillin and recited a brief prayer. If the SS had discovered us, they would have no doubt murdered us on the spot.

One evening on our march back to camp, we discovered potatoes on the ground. Some inmates in the front of the line passed word back to us that this time it was a trick and that we must not pick up the potatoes. But we were starving, and so we disregarded their warning. We hid the potatoes as best we could inside our jackets and then tucked the jackets into our pants. Upon our arrival, the camp commander — a Nazi officer we called Come-Come behind his back — shouted at us, "*Hende hoch* (lift up your arms)!" When we did, all the potatoes fell to the ground. A circle of Nazis immediately surrounded us, each of them with a stick in one hand and a leash restraining a snarling German shepherd in the other. We were told that, at the count of three, we must try to escape the circle. The Nazis swung their clubs back and forth continuously and urged their dogs to bite as many of us as possible. I made it, but I have a permanent scar on my right leg from this. Some inmates were killed in this "game."

The reason we called the camp commander Come-Come was that he seemed to have a fetish about our wooden shoes. If he noticed that a prisoner had rundown shoes, he would call to him, "Come, come! Come, come!" and this is how he got his nickname. Then, when the prisoner came close to him, Come-Come would give him a push backward, and the prisoner would fall on his back, much to his captor's delight.

One fall morning, Come-Come announced that we would be excused from work that day, plus we would be served a special meal. We could not believe our ears and questioned the motive behind this leniency. Breakfast and lunch were the same as usual, but supper was rumored to be a real meal. I wondered to myself, *What trick has the twisted Nazi mind devised now?*

One of the inmates concluded that this day was Yom Kippur, the Jewish New Year and a daylong fast. In a show of spiritual resistance, six of us refused to eat the supper. We heard the Nazis remark, "*Diese verfluchten Juden haben zich entzagt tsu fressen* (These cursed Jews, they refuse to eat even though they are starving)!"

In one camp, there was an older Nazi who did not eat lunch with the other guards, preferring to sit close to the prisoners. When no one was looking, he would share part of his sandwich with one of us. I do not know who he was or why he did this. I am certain, however, that G-d has taken him under His wing.

Wherever we worked, there was always one Nazi armed with a machine gun and a dog assigned to guard each group of ten prisoners. Of course, they never called us by our names. Sometimes even calling us by our prison numbers seemed too respectful for them. Instead, they called us: *hund* (dog), *verfluchte hund* (cursed dog), and *verfluchte schwein* (cursed pig). To make it easier to identify us were we to escape, the camp barber would shave a two-inch-wide stripe down the center of our skulls each month.

The Volsberg camp is where we worked for the Akkerman Company, digging a tunnel. The rock was blasted away with dynamite while we waited against the wall of the tunnel. Many were left totally deaf by the explosions. Then we filled metal wagons with the rock debris and pushed them out of the tunnel. Also based out of that camp, I worked for the Rabbanim Company where even heavier work was assigned as a punishment to prisoners, especially the rabbis. Here, we dug sewers. Every day, each inmate was required to dig an area of six feet long by six feet deep by two feet wide with a pick and shovel.

One day, and I will never forget this incident, there was a building in the Volsberg camp that the Nazis called a hospital. Actually, there never was a hospital in any of the camps I was in. This was just a building that they called the hospital where people who were sick or injured could go, but there was no real medical treatment provided. I glanced at my brother one morning during tzel appell to get his attention, and then I whispered to him. But, of course, how could I talk? Would I not be shot? When you are under these conditions, you learn how to speak without moving your lips or your face. So I said to my brother, "I decided to go to the hospital over there."

"Are you crazy?" he said. "You know you won't last more than two or three days there." The Nazis wanted you to work every day. If you were so sick that you couldn't work for more than two or three days, they would shoot you. "Why do you want to do that?" Sandor asked.

"I don't want to go there for a long time. Just for one day. I'm sick and tired mentally, physically, and emotionally."

"But you just can't go to the Nazis and tell them you are sick. They know that trick."

"I know," I sighed. "I was just dreaming."

Within a few days, however, I came up with a plan. I was fed up with this miserable existence. This was not living. I knew that I would never escape, so why suffer? Get it over with. Without giving it a lot of thought, I decided to commit suicide and quickly devised a plan that I confided to my brother one night while we lay next to each other in the barracks. "When the guard turns his back tomorrow," I said softly, "I will climb a tree and jump down on a rock."

"*You* are going to climb a tree?" he teased. I was never athletic. However, at the first opportunity the next day, I did manage to shimmy up a nearby tree.

A Nazi guard soon discovered that a prisoner was missing, and then he spotted me in the tree. "Come down, verfluchte hund!" he screamed. I hesitated for just a moment, then closed my eyes and jumped. I hit the rock and bounced off, suffering only minor bruises. I was extremely disappointed.

The German soldiers didn't say one word about the incident. They simply ordered me back to work. I was in a great deal of pain, but I worked there the rest of the day. When we arrived back at camp, the Nazi who had been guarding my work detail during the day went to Come-Come and said something to him — undoubtedly about what I had tried to do.

The following morning during tzel appell, Come-Come shouted, "37276, out!" I stepped out of the line and turned to face him. Without explanation, he said to me, "You are being assigned to the Housedorf camp." Housedorf was well known as a punishment camp. I didn't get a chance to say goodbye to Sandor. I never saw him again. From what I could piece together later, he died in a labor camp during an Allied bombing raid, but that was never confirmed.

Several other prisoners and I were accused of some infractions of the rules. We were marched several kilometers to Housedorf where, upon our arrival, a Nazi SS officer came up to me and said, "I will be your supervisor today." He wasn't smiling. I was ordered to chip away at a mountain for the next ten hours using only a little shovel. If I stopped even for just a moment, he hit me. If I took a deep breath, he hit me. And that went on all day. No lunch for me. Not even the dirty water.

Before we returned to camp that night, a Nazi ordered me to help him saw some wood. It was wintertime, and the Nazis needed wood for the stoves in their barracks. There was a long saw, the kind with handles at both ends. I was at one end of this saw and the Nazi at the other end. I had worked hard all day, I had been beaten constantly, and I had not eaten. I could not keep my hand steady, and my end of the saw began to shake. He started hitting me as hard as he could. At that point, I began to talk back at him. *After all, what did I have to lose? Only my life. Is it worth it? Enough was enough!*

I dropped my end of the saw and said to him, "May I say something?"

"Go ahead, dog."

"When you Nazis took me away from home, I was nineteen years old. I was a student. I have no profession. I did not eat today.

"However," and I pointed at him, "your profession is a woodchopper. And you *fressed* three times today." In German, you say *essen*, meaning to eat. But I used the word *fressen*, which means to eat like an animal devouring food. So I said to him in anger, "*Du hast gefressen drei mahl haite* (You shoved in food three times)!" He struck back at my insult, slamming my left leg behind the knee with a large tree limb.

I was out! When I awoke, I found myself back in the so-called hospital in Wustewaltersdorf, the second camp I had been in. I looked around and realized that I couldn't move. My leg was wrapped in bandages. I lay there crippled and in pain. *G-d, you really work wonders! A few weeks ago, I said I wanted to be in a hospital, and here I am. But, of course, not under these circumstances*

German soldiers checked the patients each morning. After a day or two, if there was no sign of recovery, they would simply murder the person. On the second morning, I thought, "Is it my turn to die?"

After two nights of staying there, a Nazi came to me and said, "Follow me." I couldn't walk, so I was given crutches. I didn't know what to do with them. Do the crutches go first? Or do my legs go first? I didn't know. I had never been on crutches before. Finally, they showed me what to do.

I made it into another room. My pants were tight because my leg was so swollen. The Nazi ordered me to remove my pants. I couldn't. So he took a pair of scissors or a knife, I do not remember which, and made an opening in my pant leg. I stared down. My leg looked like a rainbow, all colors. The Nazi made me lie face down on a bench. He made several deep cuts under my knee and let the pus and blood drain out. The pain was so excruciating that I began to see brilliant flashing lights, and then I once again passed out. I woke up back in the hospital ward. I started counting the days. Quite a few days went by, and they didn't kill me.

One of the patients there was a young man from Romania by the name of Feierwerker. When his entire family was murdered, he went berserk. Somehow he managed to find a razor blade. One night, he sliced off his penis and he bled to death. The Nazis were furious. They had to blame someone and, for some reason, I became the scapegoat. They claimed that I was an accomplice to this mutilation and premature death. It was obvious they felt only they had the right to do the killing.

Early the next morning, I heard my number blared out over the loudspeaker, "37276, raus!" Almost immediately, two SS came into the infirmary and dragged me outside in front of a few hundred prisoners standing at tzel appell. I blinked my eyes in the early sun, and then I saw the gallows that had been constructed there. I was led up the short flight of steps to the gallows and ordered to stand on a small stool. A coarse rope noose was tightened around my neck. I had no time to think or fear. I just stood there with this rope around my neck, staring into the blank faces of my fellow prisoners.

"Do you know why you are being hanged?" demanded Come-Come.

"Yes, I know!"

"Why?"

"Because I am a Jew, and it is a crime to be a Jew."

"Do you have a last wish before you are hanged?" Come-Come asked.

"Not a wish, but a statement and a question. I want you to know that G-d in heaven is looking down now and sees what is happening, and I want you to know that you Nazis will not get away with it.

"Now my question," I continued. "Do you have a wife?"

"Yes, I have."

"Do you have children?"

"Yes, I have children."

"Perhaps you have a dog, too?"

"Yes, I have a dog."

"When you go home every night from murdering innocent people here, how can you show love to your wife, your children, and your dog?"

"My wife is a human being. My children are human beings. Also, my dog is a human being compared to you!" Come-Come was screaming now. I was having a "nice" conversation with him. I say it was nice because he was getting so angry. It was strangely satisfying.

"And what am I?" I asked.

"You are a worm."

"Thank you for the compliment. I know my time has come to die and meet my Maker. I am ready."

Then Come-Come called for Oscar to come over. "Kick the bench away from under him!" he ordered.

"What? Me kill another Jew? Never!" Oscar vehemently refused to comply.

"Then you will no longer be a Kapo!" the red-faced Nazi screamed, ripping the badge of rank from his chest.

"I don't want to be a Kapo."

Come-Come then turned to Schreiber, Oscar's assistant, and ordered him to kick the bench. Schreiber also refusing to obey, approached the commander, his badge already in his hand. Outraged, Come-Come walked over and kicked the bench with all of his strength, and I dropped like a rock. The rope snapped! I lay on the ground, stunned but quite alive!

Come-Come, looking startled and even somewhat embarrassed, reached down to shake my hand, "Congratulations, dog. According to international law, you cannot be punished twice for the same crime."

I don't remember if I shook his hand or not, but I do remember replying, "I did not know you Nazis were bound by any kind of law, especially international law."

Orders were given to take me away and put me back into the infirmary.

I knew at once that G-d had intervened on my behalf. I knew I could now survive anything. As a matter of fact, I knew at that moment I must survive! Death as an escape was no longer an option. G-d ordained that I live, therefore I must live a life dedicated to Him and the fulfillment of His commandments.

VIDDUI — A CONFESSION

For forty years, I have related this incident with one fabricated element. In the past, I explained that I was condemned to be hanged because of a poem against Adolph Hitler that I had written while in the camp hospital. I confess that I found it too embarrassing to tell the true facts behind this episode. I apologize for this falsehood.

Chapter 8

A SHOWCASE CAMP

I did not receive any medical treatment for my broken leg in the infirmary. Left untreated, it healed in a bent position, and I became a cripple, able to move about only with the aid of crutches.

By January 1945, the Allies were closing in on the German armies. Our captors were becoming nervous and began evacuating all the prisoners from the camp. They wanted to destroy any evidence that the death camps had ever existed. For some reason that only G-d knows, I alone was removed from the infirmary and transported by truck to the Durnhau, a camp erected on a large field not far from Breslau, Germany. All of the patients left behind most probably were murdered in their beds.

The infirmary at Durnhau was a large, wooden building that housed about 100 people, mostly the infirm and crippled. We were confined to the three tiers of bunks which lined the walls. We slept on bare, wooden planks without benefit of mattress or even straw. Since most of us were crippled, we did not have to endure the tzel appells.

The meals were better than I had eaten in any of the other camps. For both breakfast and lunch, we were served some kind of cooked buckwheat called kasha. (Since the war, I cannot even look at kasha, but my wife loves it. So, for her sake, I eat it with my eyes closed.) For supper, we were usually given two slices of bread and a vegetable stew which, by comparison to what we had been eating in the other camps, was actually quite delicious. Almost as important as the food was that we did not have to stand in line to receive our rations. We were served right in our barracks.

In this camp, there was an actual four-hole outhouse instead of a latrine. Not very luxurious, I'll agree, but it's interesting how the smallest improvements could seem so important after the horrors of the concentration camp.

None of us was required to work. Instead, we spent the long days sharing our experiences with one another and in prayer.

On several occasions, the Nazis escorted civilians around the camp and through our quarters. I assumed that these people were Red Cross observers whom the Nazis wanted to impress with their humane treatment of their prisoners. Durnhau was probably a "showcase" camp. The Nazis ordered us not to speak to these visitors. I was never really close enough to communicate with them anyway. They would stop briefly at the doorway of our barracks and then be ushered along by the German soldiers.

I often wondered why the SS had not killed me. Certainly they could have done so at any time. Slowly came the realization that the Almighty held me in His hand. He had ordained that, for whatever reason, I live. I expressed my thankfulness to my G-d in my daily prayers.

A Greek Jew was lying in the bed next to mine. I couldn't speak Greek, and he could speak neither Hungarian nor Yiddish. Mostly we communicated with hand signals. He did manage, however, to teach me one word, "lookie-lookie." He used this word whenever he wanted to get my attention.

Near midnight on May 9, 1945, the door to the infirmary opened very slowly. Two armed men in strange uniforms crept in quietly. My Greek friend poked me and pointed. "Lookie-lookie!" he whispered hoarsely.

"We are Russians," the two men said in broken German. "The war is over! Who can handle a rifle?" they asked. A few of us volunteered. I had received quite a bit of training with rifles as a youth in levente back in Hungary. During a marksmanship contest one summer, I had scored among the highest. Now I had the opportunity to practice what I had learned. I wanted to take part in my own liberation.

"Where are the Nazi headquarters?" they asked. We pointed it out to them. "Hit them as they come running out!" the Russians ordered. The Nazis did not have a guard posted outside their barracks. They thought that their crippled Jewish prisoners could do no them no harm. They were wrong.

I lay on my stomach and aimed the rifle at the door of the headquarters. There were only five or six Russian soldiers. They fired into the headquarters building and the Nazis ran out, still in their pajamas We all started shooting. Since it was dark, I have no idea whether or not I hit any of them. Within minutes, it was all over. I saw some Nazis lying dead or wounded on the ground and others being taken prisoner by the Russians. The Nazis were routed, and we were free!

Free? Now what? Shall we cry? Shall we sing?

The war was over. That fact, however, brought with it no particular reason to rejoice. I was without parents, home, or family. I was a crippled, emaciated shell of the young man I once was. I could look in a mirror and see only a stranger. I had nothing but questions.

Why had I survived, but not my parents? Could I go on living with these thoughts? Freedom? What a joke.

Chapter 9

AFTER THE HOLOCAUST

Although I was free, I had lost the zest, if not the will, to live. I was crippled and alone, without parents, without home or country, without money. The Russians kept asking me where I wanted to go, and I truly didn't know or even care.

"I want to go back to Hungary," I finally replied. Why? Because I had to go someplace. Two kindly Russian soldiers volunteered to take me from Durnhau to a hospital in Budapest. After a few days there, I was transferred to a hospital in Debrecen, which was the closest city with medical facilities to my hometown of Nyíradony.

Almost daily, the newspapers of Central Europe printed lists of the names of Jews who had survived the war. Three days after I was transferred to this hospital, my brother walked into my ward. Dezso was alive! I hadn't seen Dezso since his last visit home from the labor camp, and that was several months before the Nazis invaded Nyíradony. He had found my name on one of these lists.

You cannot imagine our reunion. We could not speak. We just cried, for we never dreamed that we would ever be reunited. I was certain that he must have been murdered, and he thought the same about me. He didn't know if anybody from our family had survived the Holocaust.

Dezso wanted to know everything that happened to our parents, to me, and to the other members of our family. He demanded to know every detail. With much anguish, I told him how we were forced from our home, about our imprisonment in our own synagogue and in the ghetto, about Sandor and about seeing Margit and her children, about Auschwitz and the gas chambers and the crematorium, about the labor camps. The whole story. With the long pauses of reflection and of tears, it took several hours to relate.

It was now Dezso's turn. He told me that he had spent nearly the entire war in one slave labor camp after another. From the time he was taken from our home in September 1942, he was shunted from Hungary to Romania and back to Hungary and forced to work at such labor as breaking stones and hauling lumber up mountains. In March 1945, he was taken by cattle car to the Mauthausen concentration camp in Austria. Fortunately, the war ended shortly thereafter, and he was freed by the U.S. Army on May 5, 1945.

Immediately after the war, he returned to Hungary where he pored over the newspapers every day hoping for some sign that he was not the only member of our family to have survived. Dezso told me that when he discovered my name on the list, he left immediately to try to find me. His very presence there in the hospital ward sparked within me renewed courage and a reason to live.

My brother could stay with me in the hospital for only a couple of days. He was on his way to Szaszregen, Romania, where he had had a girlfriend before the war. Her name was Marika Langsner, and she had also been in Auschwitz and in several labor camps. Dezso had learned that she survived the war and was on her way home to Romania. I understood that he wanted to find her, but it was very difficult to say goodbye to my brother and to be alone once again. We promised to stay in touch.

In the weeks to come, the physicians in Debrecen operated on my left leg several times with no success. Finally, in desperation, they recommended that the limb be amputated. "If I can't have both my legs, I don't want to live!" I shouted.

"Listen to the doctors," Dezso wrote in a letter in an effort to convince me. "You can live a normal life. Look around you — look at all the injured from the war. One leg, no legs, one arm, no arms. You will learn to walk again." At the time, I weighed all of thirty-eight kilograms (eighty-four pounds). I was skin and bones. I had my doubts.

One afternoon, a different doctor came into my room. I remember that he was quite short and that he spoke in broken Hungarian. "Son," he said, "let me try one more surgery." His accent was quite pronounced. I asked if he was German. "Yes, I am a German," he replied.

"Don't you dare touch my leg!" I cried. Understandably, I didn't trust any German surgeons at that time.

"Listen, son," he said to me, trying to quiet my fears, "I was a German, not a Nazi. Yes, I am a German and a Christian. I worked against Hitler. I, too, was imprisoned in a concentration camp. I'm here to help you. Let me try one more surgery."

"What will you do?" I pleaded.

"Quite honestly, I won't know until we get there."

"When you put me to sleep, you can cut off my leg. You could cut off my head — I wouldn't know," I argued. "I will let you do this on one condition. I want you to sign a paper explaining that I am not granting permission for *any* amputation!"

"Of course, I will," he replied, shaking his head in disbelief at my stubbornness. I wrote out the agreement in Hungarian, and the doctor signed it. Then I handed it to the nurse for safekeeping. The nurse's name was Esther and the German word for nurse is *krankenschwester* or *schwester* for short. So I said, "Schwester Esther, do a favor for me, will you please? Take this paper and keep it for me until I wake up. They are going to perform another surgery. However, I do not give them permission to amputate my leg."

The next morning, I was wheeled into the operating room, and they put me under. I have no idea how long the operation lasted, but the first question I asked when I woke up was, "Do I still have my leg?"

"Yes, you do," a nurse answered.

I expected to see a cast but there was no cast. Starting to panic, I reached down for my leg, but couldn't find it. A huge pillow covered it.

The doctor walked in and saw what I was doing. He smiled and said, "Yes, you have your leg. As a matter of fact, I want you to move your toes." I moved my toes. In my excitement, in fact, I lifted up my whole leg.

"Wow, that's a big toe you have there," the doctor laughed. "You're going to be okay."

After a few days, he put a wire through my knee and rigged me up to a machine that pulled my leg up and down over and over again as I lay there. A few days later, the machine was disconnected, and the doctor told me to get out of bed and walk. I was so weak that I couldn't even get out of bed, let alone get around by myself. Two nurses helped me from my bed and held onto my arms and I walked!

"You are limping," the doctor said.

"I am?"

"Yes, you are. Come back here to me," he instructed. He measured both my legs and concluded, "After so many surgeries, your left leg is now shorter than the right one. You have a choice."

"What choice?" I questioned.

"We can stretch the shorter leg, or we can push the right one back a bit to make them even," he explained.

'What? I don't believe you." I stared at him in disbelief.

"Yes," he said. "A person's limb can be pulled or pushed."

"That is very interesting. But do you know what, Doctor? I want you to leave my right leg alone. As for my left one, you want to push it or pull it, do whatever you think is necessary."

The next day, he put me in a cast from my neck down to my toes. It was at least three weeks before the cast was removed. In August 1945, after two more weeks of therapy and with the aid of crutches, I was able to walk out of the hospital. Two male nurses were kind enough to give me a ride in their jeep to Nyíradony.

They dropped me off at the outskirts of town, and I began walking up the familiar dirt street toward my house. It had changed very little. The windows of my father's store were now boarded up, and our dogs were no longer in the side yard but, when I peeked over the fence, I saw the two peach trees and the two plum trees still growing there. I wanted to reconnect with whatever memories of my childhood might still be lingering there within the walls of our home, so I knocked on the door.

A man answered. He introduced me to an elderly lady who was now living in our house. When I explained to this wonderful non-Jewish woman that this was my family's house before the war, she apologized profusely and said she would make arrangements to move out as soon as she found another place to live. In just a few days, I was able to move into the home of my youth.

I wrote Dezso and asked him to come back to Nyíradony. He had married Marika, and toward the end of September, they moved in with me. Our childhood house provided some comfort, but everything else had been stolen by the Nazis and by some of the townspeople. The three of us had very little money but were able to scrape up enough cash to buy the bare necessities.

I was able to locate only about four or five others who had survived the war and returned home to Nyíradony. Nearly all the rest of our

Jewish community had perished. I was able to find my old friend, Sanyi Gelberger, and two of the three Weinberger boys, the sons of the shochet. I also found two other brothers by the name of Gelberger. But that was all. We did not even have a minyan, the minimum of ten men necessary for a service.

"Are you still alive?" one of my former neighbors exclaimed in amazement at seeing me walking down the street one day. I hoped I was mistaken, but I sensed a bit of disappointment in his voice. He expressed regret at what had happened, but seemed anxious to put some distance between us. I knew from personal experience that many Hungarians were as responsible as the Nazis for murdering my parents and nearly my entire family. About 140 of my relatives were gone, lost to me forever. I felt bitter and lost. There were far too many painful memories for me, and I simply couldn't handle it any longer.

"I am going to leave this country," I told my brother. "I have read about a camp in Germany for survivors of the war. It's called a Displaced Persons camp. From there, I can go to another country. I want to go to Israel, the U.S., or even Canada. I don't care. I just have to get out of here."

My brother tried talking me out of my plan. He told me I should not go by myself, that I should wait because I was still walking with crutches. But I had made up my mind. I did not want to wait. He suggested that I talk with Sanyi and that perhaps he would travel with me to help me. I did, and he agreed. Sanyi and I left Nyíradony in October 1945. Dezso and Marika remained behind in Nyíradony until the following summer.

In order to get from Nyíradony to the DP camp at Bergen-Belsen, we first had to travel by train to Budapest. There were transports each day from Budapest to Vienna, Austria, and eventually on to Bergen-Belsen. While in Budapest, we stayed in one of the several buildings provided by the Jewish community for those waiting to leave the country. We waited in Budapest for what seemed an eternity. We were anxious to get moving. Actually, we were only there about ten days, but every day dragged on and on we were so impatient.

I was still finding it very difficult to face each new day. I continued to dwell on the misfortunes that had befallen me and my family until finally I was drawn once again to the realization that surely G-d was holding my hand. He had held my hand so often during the gloom and despair and the atrocities of the camps. During these times, it was often very difficult to praise and thank G-d. In some remote corner of my heart, however, I always knew that He would come — and He did. Of course, everyone asks why did it take Him so long? I believe I have a possible answer. G-d was waiting for the people of the free world to wake up and take action. When nobody did, G-d finally cried, "Enough is enough."

Our turn finally came, and Sanyi and I were on our way to Vienna.

PART TWO

Chapter 10

JOURNEY FROM THE ASHES

Hundreds and hundreds of Jewish refugees from all over Europe were converging in Vienna. We were all housed in the Rothchild Hospital, a huge building where we again waited and waited. It soon became apparent that the people who had money were the first to leave for the DP camp in Germany. Others less fortunate had to wait their turn. And so Sanyi and I bided our time. At least by then, I was able to abandon my crutches.

After four weeks, I had had enough. I went to the person who was responsible for assigning the people for transfer to the DP camp. When I met with him I said, "Listen, there are people who just came here and they have left already."

"Wait your turn," he demanded.

I had used up all my patience long before I ever got to him. By now, I was yelling at him. All the while, there was an elderly person, a Hungarian by the name of Mr. Winkler whom I'd met in Vienna, who was taking it all in. He said to me, "After you are through with this gentleman, I want to talk to you." So we made an appointment for later in the day.

When we met, he said to me, "Tomorrow, I am in the next group of refugees who are leaving this building for the train station. I can't help you get in this group, but if you can get on the train, then I can help you."

Early the next morning, the group assembled outside the Rothchild Hospital. I found Sanyi and said to him, "Come with me. We are going to the train station."

"But we don't have transfers. Without transfers, we can't even get into the station!" he cried.

"Don't worry," I said. "We'll figure out something."

When the papers of everyone in the group had been checked, a leader began marching them the two kilometers to the train station. I said to Sanyi, "Let's go!"

And so we went, following along as close as we dared. But, because of my limp, we soon fell far behind. "Grab my arm," Sanyi urged, "we're not going to make it!" We were both out of breath when we arrived. We stopped next to the guard at the gates of the train station.

"Oh, please let us in. Our transport is inside. We belong with that group," we pleaded. The guard let us in, and we approached the train but waited until the group from the Rothchild Hospital was on board. Yanek, one of the group leaders, saw us. He asked us how we got there and where were we going.

"It is really none of your business," I answered. "This train takes all kinds of people everywhere."

"You are not going with my group," he replied.

"Who said we are going with your group?" I snapped back. "We are just going."

We quickly boarded the train, but not the same railroad car as the transport group. Sanyi and I had just settled into our seats when the two leaders, Yanek and his friend, approached us. They asked again, "Where do you think you are going?"

"We are going to Germany!" I answered with determination.

"You are not going with our group," Yanek insisted.

"And who said we are?" I barked back.

"You two are going to get into big trouble!" They tried to throw us off the train. The two of them grabbed us and started pushing us. I was standing near one door and my friend was at the other. As they tried to push us off the train, my friend became hysterical. I yelled to him, "Hold on to the railing, Sanyi! Hold on tight!"

The train was about to go over a bridge where British soldiers were stationed at one end and American soldiers at the other. The train was moving quite slowly as the military police prepared to board to check the immigrants' papers. I looked up and noticed the emergency brake handle. I told my friend, "I am going to pull the brake, if I can reach it. Then we must jump!" Just before the train reached the bridge, I pulled the brake and we jumped off the train and rolled down into a sandbank. The train stopped abruptly.

The MPs came quickly. "What is going on here?" they questioned.

"They wanted to throw us off the train," we explained. "We want to go to the Bergen-Belsen DP camp. We have both waited several weeks in Vienna, but since we have no money, they kept us there." The leaders are taking bribes from some refugees on the train," I told them.

"Are you sure?" the MPs asked.

"I am positive!"

The officers led us back onto the train and escorted the two of us along with the two transport leaders into a car crowded with about a hundred men and women. The passengers soon realized what was happening.

One of the passengers in the car was Mr. Winkler. He whispered to me in Hungarian, "Don't worry, I am going to help you now." He, too, was upset with the two leaders since he was forced to bribe them for a place on the train. He told me to stand close to him and he would tell me which of the people had also paid for their seats on the train, especially those he felt would not remember the false names under which they were traveling.

Mr. Winkler kept his face in the newspaper as he cued me quietly in Hungarian, "The lady wearing the white scarf on her head."

"Could you please let me see your passport?" I asked her in Yiddish. "What is your name?" Because I spoke in Yiddish, she dropped her guard and gave her real name, not the one on the passport she was carrying.

While this exchange was taking place, Mr. Winkler gave me six other names. Almost without exception, they gave their real names. The scam was exposed and the group's leaders, including Yanek and his assistant, were immediately arrested.

"Here are all the refugees' papers. You will take them to Iring, an outpost where members of the Bricha will meet you," the MP instructed my friend and me. We were told there was an organization called the Irgun Zeva'i Le'ummi (IZL), the Hebrew Struggle for National Liberation, informally known as the Jewish Underground Armed Organization. The word *bricha* means selected. The Bricha was a group of people selected from the IZL for special missions.

After this incident, however, Sanyi began having second thoughts about leaving Europe. He remained off the train and eventually made his way back to Nyíradony. That left me in charge of the group until we arrived at Iring, where we were welcomed by the Bricha leader, Menachem Begin.

"Where is Yanek?" Begin asked with a puzzled look. I told him what had transpired on the train. With a look of obvious disgust, Begin took charge and began giving instructions.

The post-war government of Germany was divided roughly into thirds and controlled by the Russians, the British, and the Americans. Relations among the three were often strained. We were in the Russian zone and needed to cross over into the American-held sector to continue our journey to Bergen-Belsen. The Americans were reluctant to assist refugees wanting to get out of the Russian zone. We had to do so at our own risk.

"In a few nights, when the moon will be dark, we will cross the border into the American-held sector," Begin told us. "At times, it will be necessary to crawl on the ground so no one will spot us. When there are searchlights, everyone must lie flat on the ground and remain motionless. The final part of the journey will be through a tunnel."

There were about twenty in our group. Each of us had recently survived unthinkable terrors. Although there was certainly danger in our plan, none of us could feel anything but excitement and anticipation. We waited in Iring until one night Begin gave the order to move out. Although harrowing, this particular ordeal was relatively uneventful, and we were welcomed by the American military into its sector. Begin then returned to Iring. Our group was just one of many that Begin would lead to safety and eventual emigration. His eventual role of leadership in Israel was due in no small part to the heroism he displayed as the Bricha leader.

On a bitterly cold day in December 1945, our group boarded the train for the trip to Hanover in northern Germany, where we switched trains and rode to the town of Celle. We were now only about thirty kilometers from Bergen-Belsen. The DP camp sent trucks to meet every group of refugees arriving in Celle. I had to wait only a short time before I, too, was on my way to Bergen-Belsen.

The Bergen-Belsen DP camp was located adjacent to a former Nazi concentration camp. This concentration camp, the first to be liberated by the Allies, was taken by the British in April 1945, and the DP camp there continued to be under the British command, with our rations being provided by the Americans. I had mixed feelings about being so close to such a place. Knowing that so many Jews had died there at the hands of the Nazis was quite unnerving. On the other hand, I felt proud to have survived the butchery and to be standing now on the ashes of the Third Reich preparing to begin a future the Nazis would have denied me.

Yosele Rosensaft, head administrator of the DP camp, welcomed us upon our arrival. As there were many single Orthodox men and women registering with the Jewish camp committee, we decided to request two buildings for our group. We were assigned to buildings L-2 and L-6 in the area called Lager 4. We called the men's building *Ts'ire Agudas Yisrael* (Young Religious Jews) and the women's building *Beis Yaakov* (House of Jacob). A young man by the name of Leib Gantz and I were named joint administrators of the buildings.

One of the first things I did upon my arrival at the camp was apply for permission to emigrate to Israel, the United States, and Canada, whichever would accept me first. I was anxious to leave the still anti-Semitic environs of Europe. As refugees, however, we had no choice but to wait patiently.

Although our basic needs were being met, we lacked a place to fulfill our spiritual needs. The camp's Jewish Central Committee granted us permission to build a synagogue and supplied us with some used lumber. They even arranged for us to receive a Sefer Torah, the scroll of the Pentateuch that is kept in the ark of the synagogue and read week by week during services.

Every Friday, our organization rented a truck to carry flour to a bakery in Celle to bake challah for Sabbath. I traveled with the driver and eventually learned to drive the truck myself. In Celle, I acted as the *mashgiach*, supervising the bakery to make certain that it was kosher. Each week, I returned to camp with hundreds of small warm rolls.

There were probably close to 2,000 refugees in this camp. One day as I was walking down the street with a friend, Fishel Wiesel, I spotted a man I thought I knew. "Fishel," I said, "this man looks familiar to me. I think I know who he is." I quickly crossed the street and approached him.

"Are you Oscar?" I asked.

"Oscar who?"

"I don't know your last name," I said. "But are you Oscar?"

"No, I am not."

"Why are you afraid? Why are you not telling me the truth? You *are* Oscar!"

"What do you know about Oscar?" he inquired.

"Oscar, in one camp where you were the Kapo, I was heading for the latrine in the middle of night. And, when you saw me, you hit me and said, 'Can't you see the Nazi up there? He'll shoot you because he'll think you're trying to escape. You know we're not allowed to use the latrines at night!' That was one incident. And do you remember when they hanged a Jew? And they called you over to kick the bench?"

"Yes, I do remember," he answered quietly.

"Oscar, that was me!"

He took me in his arms and cried bitterly. He said to me, "Help me."

"What can I do for you?"

"You know how the people felt toward the Kapos. They felt we were all traitors. It's not true. They won't let us leave this camp."

"I'll help you," I assured him.

He and I walked directly over to the Jewish Central Committee, where I told the officials there what Oscar had done to try to save my life. A lawyer there wrote up an affidavit about the incident, and I signed it. The officials notarized it and gave it to Oscar. He then had the documents he needed to get out of the camp.

One of my responsibilities as an administrator for our group was to pick up our rations from the Americans, although the DP camp was in the British zone, and the British had their offices in the former Nazi headquarters. On one of these twice-weekly errands, I met an English soldier named David who struck up a conversation with me. He was Jewish and spoke fluent Yiddish and we soon became the best of friends. I'm not certain I ever knew his last name; everyone just called him by his first name.

Over the ensuing months, I came to rely on David for many different things, including help in translating letters for some of the refugees who were trying to locate family members. It was David who suggested that I wear a British uniform when visiting his headquarters so I could move about more freely and not have to answer so many questions from his superiors. The memory of my friendship with David is one of the many highlights of the time I spent in the DP camp.

Eventually, Bergen-Belsen developed into a thriving community with barbers, shoemakers, kosher butchers, all kinds of stores. In time and with the generous assistance of the United Nations Relief and Rehabilitation Administration (UNRRA), most of our necessities were available in the camp. Although it was a refugee camp, it was the first semblance of a true community life that many of us enjoyed since before the war.

It was customary to produce biblical plays during the holiday of Purim, the Feast of Esther. Our group presented the *Selling of Joseph*, and I played the role of Yehudah, the fourth son of Jacob. There were also regular classes and religious studies in the camp. All these activities helped time go by as we waited for a country to open up for us.

One Friday in Celle, I was told about the Hanover Music Conservatory, which was about sixty kilometers from our camp. From then on, I took music and voice lessons there twice a month.

Generally, each Jewish organization in the camp held its own religious services on Sabbath and holidays. For the High Holidays, two large services were conducted for those people who did not belong to any organization. I conducted services for one of those groups in a large hall for the next two years. Our group held daily services as well.

Also at the same time, although I am not certain how it came about, I was called to the port city of Bremen to lead High Holiday services for both the local Jewish community and the American soldiers stationed there.

One day, I tried to be a *shadchan* (matchmaker) in the DP camp. Rabbi Abraham Blobstein, our spiritual leader, said to me, "I would like your help in finding a wife for my son." Shortly thereafter, another man approached me and asked if I could find a *zivig*, a marriage partner, for his child. Excited, I made a few contacts, and within a few weeks, arrangements were made for the two prospective *mechutonim* (future in-laws) to meet. When they got together, they spoke glowingly about their respective *yichus* (family backgrounds and pedigrees).

After a lengthy discussion, the two young people were invited to meet. What a comedy of errors. The two youngsters were both boys! I had been so elated that a match could be made so easily that I did not think to ask. I wanted to crawl into a hole.

One day in the fall of 1948, I spotted a notice that was posted outside the Central Committee office that announced Canada was accepting tailors. Since I knew a little tailoring, I applied and was approved. After four long years in the DP camp, I would soon be on my way to Montreal.

Chapter 11

COMING TO NORTH AMERICA

The *General Langfit* docked in Halifax, Nova Scotia, on the Thursday before *slichot*, the special service held at midnight on the Saturday preceding Rosh Hashanah. We had boarded the ship, a 200-foot freighter, in Bremerhaven, Germany, after a short train ride from Celle. As we left the harbor, the captain requested that I chant the memorial prayer for the souls of our murdered brothers and sisters, mothers and fathers.

As I chanted the *Kel Maley Rachamim*, my voice reverberated off the steel walls of the hull, creating echoes that washed back over us as so many memories of the souls we had lost. Everyone, myself included, stood there in the hold of this old ship, mesmerized by the sounds of the moment. And then the silence filled with so much meaning.

Many of us spent the entire two-week trip nauseated by the diesel fumes and the rolling and pitching of the ship as it crossed the North Atlantic. The *General Langfit* was essentially a metal box designed to transport cargo. The ship's hold this time, however, was filled with hundreds of Jewish refugees lying on the floor. The Americans supplied us with food. Cereal. Boxes and boxes of cereal.

How eerily similar it seemed for so many Jews to be thrown together with no place to sleep, contained in a vessel under the control of a foreign nation and steaming inexorably toward an uncertain future. Yet how wonderfully different. We were here this time by choice. By the grace of G-d, we were once again in control of our lives, our destiny. We were free!

Not wanting to travel on the Sabbath, Joe Fishman — a good friend of mine from the DP camp — and I chose not to continue the trip from Halifax to Montreal until Sunday. The leaders of the Halifax

Jewish community and the Hebrew Immigrant Aid Society offered us tea and cakes as they welcomed us to the shores of Canada.

The president of the Baron DeHirsh Synagogue, a large Orthodox congregation, was also there to greet us. He insisted that Joe and I stay with him and his family. His wife was an excellent cook, and hers was the first genuine Sabbath dinner I had enjoyed since I was taken from my home by the Nazis in the spring of 1944. The food in the DP camp had been good enough, but despite our best efforts, we could not replicate the true atmosphere of a Jewish home on the Sabbath. I was torn between absorbing the closeness of this special event and of this loving Jewish family and recalling my own childhood experiences — coming home from synagogue with my father and brothers and finding my mother and sister resplendent in their white Sabbath dresses. How long would the pain of memories that could never be re-created continue? For a lifetime, I expected.

Before midnight Saturday, we went to the synagogue for the slichot. The rabbi there had engaged a cantor from Montreal, and he was to fly into Halifax for the High Holidays. The assembled congregation waited expectantly for his arrival. All eyes were on the door. Some even went outside to look down the avenue for his taxi, but the cantor never arrived. In desperation, the rabbi asked, "Is there anyone here who can chant the slichot prayers?"

Joe Fishman opened his big mouth. "My friend here is a cantor," he proclaimed. "Let him do it." The rabbi gratefully accepted. Nervously, I mounted the *bimah* in the center of synagogue. I quieted my nerves with prayers that soon took over my consciousness as I felt my voice reach out to the Lord of the Universe Himself.

When the service concluded, the synagogue committee surrounded me, insisting that I return to chant the Rosh Hashanah and Yom Kippur services. This I did. In fact, I returned the following two years to chant High Holiday services at the Baron DeHirsh Synagogue.

After two weeks in Halifax, Joe Fishman and I boarded a train for Montreal. When we arrived, the Hebrew Immigrant Aid Society handed each of us a $10 bill and a list of places available for rent. I headed for a neighborhood that seemed to have a synagogue on every block, and I found a room with Mr. & Mrs. Bomze, a kindly German-Jewish couple.

I turned my attention to finding a job, but first I badly needed a haircut. With my precious $10 bill in hand, I went to a barber. I did not realize the value of that much money in 1948. I handed the bill to the barber after my haircut, and he gave me $3 in change. I thought I had made a good deal, but later learned he had simply taken advantage of a newly arrived immigrant. The price of a haircut at that time was probably less than two dollars.

I decided to seek out the *Vaad Harabanim*, the Rabbinical Council, to find a position as a mashgiach since I felt qualified to oversee kosher practices. I was hired by the Manischewitz matzah factory twenty-five kilometers outside of Montreal in the town of Longail. The plant was in the process of baking unleavened bread for Passover.

I was elated! My wages, however, were only $80 per month, and my monthly rent was $60. It was difficult to make ends meet, but the Bomzes insisted I stay on and pay them whenever I was able. My daily diet was bread and grapes — for breakfast, lunch, and supper. That was all I could afford for a long time.

After a few days, I approached the foreman with some infractions of the kosher laws. I had seen the employees gather in a designated corner to eat lunch without removing their white coats. Sandwich crumbs clung to their coats, and they neglected to wash their hands before returning to work. Under these conditions, the matzah could not be considered strictly kosher for Passover. The foreman frowned and shouted at the workers in English, which I had yet to learn. They compliantly removed their coats, shook them out, and then gathered at the sink to wash their hands.

When I arrived home that evening, there was a message for me from the rabbi administrator saying that I needed to see him the next morning.

"I must leave early for work," I explained when I met with him.

"Never mind," he answered, "I have a different job for you." My supervision at the Manischewitz company was considered too strict, and I was being transferred to another job. The rules of *kashrut* (kosher) were obviously more lax in America.

"Thank you very much, Rabbi. But if this is what kashrut is about in America, as a mashgiach I want no part of it."

Instead of accepting the transfer, I headed for the garment district to try my hand at tailoring. I was soon hired at a company called Ackie Sanft Ladies Wear. I struggled in vain for a day or two attempting to pass myself off as a skilled tailor. It didn't work. The foreman, Moishe Lang, quickly realized that I was a mere novice. He fortunately took pity on me and suggested I begin staying after work so he could teach me some basic tailoring techniques. Back home in Hungary, I had learned to make complete garments on a sewing machine powered with a foot pedal. In this factory, we sat eight people in a row at electric machines where we made only pockets or sleeves. With his help, I mastered the art of piecework tailoring.

All new employees — most of them war refugees from Central Europe — were escorted around the factory by Mr. Sanft himself. He pompously presumed they knew nothing about modern conveniences. He would even take the newcomers to the washroom and explain in detail how to flush a toilet. I had endured this insult because I desperately needed the job.

A few weeks later, a new employee arrived. Before the work bell rang, I forewarned him about the bathroom demonstration. "No one is going to make fun of me," he exclaimed with a grin. Soon, Mr. Sanft came in to lead the new man on a tour around the plant.

Standing under the shower, Mr. Sanft began telling him how the toilet worked. At that very moment, the newcomer asked, "What is this?" as he turned on the shower. The man ran out laughing hysterically and never returned. Mr. Sanft did not show his face at the factory for two days.

After a few months, Mr. Lang suggested that I could advance my career more quickly by moving to another clothing manufacturer. He directed me to Morrwill Clothing, a company owned by three brothers in partnership. "Just tell them you've been working for Auckie Sanft," Lang told me. I followed his suggestion and was hired.

Now that I had a secure job and food on the table, I decided to further my religious studies that were interrupted in Hungary so many years ago. I was truly indebted to G-d that I was alive and well once more. I cannot say that I was completely whole because of those souls I had lost, yet I had much for which to be thankful. I registered at the Maor Hagolah Rabbinical College for evening and Sunday classes.

One Sunday morning, Irwing Wentman, one of the firm's salespeople, phoned me to ask if I would do a favor for him. I had a few free hours, so I agreed. He picked me up and we drove to the factory where he asked me to hem a piece of fabric into a scarf. I accomplished the simple task and asked no questions. Then we went into his office, and I watched as he wrapped the scarf in gift paper.

"Was this so important?" I questioned. "Couldn't you wait until tomorrow?"

"Oh, no!" he replied. "Today is Mother's Day. I am taking this scarf to my mother in the nursing home."

"How often do you visit your mother?" I asked.

"It's difficult," he replied sheepishly. "You know I have to spend a lot of time on the road. Sometimes I am gone for a week. Sometimes longer."

"I asked you a simple question, and you are telling me a whole story," I snapped. "How often do you visit your mother?"

I visit her every Mother's Day."

"What is Mother's Day?" I asked. I had never heard of it. He explained that it was a special day set aside each a year to honor mothers. I opened the package and tore the scarf in two. He was visibly upset and asked why I had done such a thing. I had visions of my wonderful mother who was so recently murdered by the Nazis while he and his family were safe in Canada.

"If you cannot find the time to visit your mother, then I don't wish to be a part of this Mother's Day gift."

He returned to his office and moments later emerged with another gift-wrapped package. "Please come with me to see my mother," he pleaded. I reluctantly agreed. When we entered his mother's room, she looked up at me and exclaimed, "*Oy, Chazen* (Oh, Cantor)!" Her son looked at me with surprise. "Do you know my mother?"

"Yes, I do. As student cantors, we take turns conducting Sabbath services each week for the elderly in the nursing home, but I did not know she was your mother." He gave his mother the gift, and her arthritic hands shook as she struggled to open the package. When at last she pulled out the two torn pieces of the scarf, I almost fainted. She looked at her son with a puzzled stare.

"This young man has taught me a valuable lesson," he said apologetically. "I am sorry that I have not visited you more often. I promise I will do better."

Two years after arriving in Montreal, I was invited to conduct Sabbath services at different synagogues on a rotating basis. I also was encouraged to continue my musical studies. One of my teachers, Cantor Eugene Goldberger, arranged for me to audition for Madame Pauline Lichtenstein — better known by her stage name of Pauline Donalda — who taught voice at McGill University in Montreal and who had sung with the great tenor Enrico Caruso.

I chanted a Hebrew prayer for her and then asked, "Do you think I have what it takes to pursue a career as a professional cantor?" She immediately accepted me as her student, although I declined at first because I could not pay for the lessons. She graciously offered to teach me at no charge. I studied with her for about four years.

Meanwhile, I worked myself up from one clothing manufacturer to another, trying to better myself. Too often, however, my bosses wanted me to work on the Sabbath. As an observant Jew, I could not comply. This frequently caused uncomfortable tension between my employers and me. My luck was about to change.

In 1955, I received a letter from the Mercantile Trust Company of St. Louis, Missouri. The letter, which had been forwarded to me from Hungary, stated that a David Fettman had died, and the bank was seeking the heirs to his estate. This man was my father's half-brother and had left Hungary before my father was born. I vaguely recalled my father mentioning him.

I sent the letter to my brother Dezso who was now living in Gary, Indiana. Several months after I left Hungary, Dezso and his wife, Marika, emigrated to the United States. We had family in Indiana, and so Dezso went to work in our Uncle Sam's laundry there. Later, he worked in the family's Five Star Supermarket with some of his cousins and shortly thereafter opened his own supermarket.

Dezso and I started searching for and verifying all living relatives. Just before the deadline, we replied to the inquiry. In February 1954 — miracle of miracles — I received the enormous sum of $1,500! That was a lot of money in those days, especially given my financial position at the time. I felt as though I was suddenly quite wealthy.

I was determined to live as an observant Jew, and now the Lord was giving me the opportunity to do so. I decided to open my own factory where I could continue to observe the Sabbath as G-d had commanded: "Observe and remember the Sabbath day to keep it holy."

Moishe Bregman, the foreman's assistant at the company where I worked, was willing to put up the rest of the necessary cash and join me as a partner in establishing a contracting shop. We did not have to make a large investment since the fabric arrived at our shop already pre-cut and ready to assemble into finished garments. We called ourselves Canada Sportswear.

One Sabbath morning as I was praying in the synagogue, a fellow congregant told me that on his way there he had noticed that my shop was open. In disbelief, I quickly removed my prayer shawl, interrupted my prayers, and left the sanctuary. I ran down the street and up the narrow stairway of our building where I discovered Moishe sorting and checking garments. In no uncertain terms, I reminded him that our contract stated that our factory would be closed every Sabbath and on all Jewish holidays. Quite angry, I turned and walked out.

The following Monday morning, I called him into my office and told him that either he had to go or I was going. He offered to buy me out on the condition that I continue to manage the shop. I felt we finally understood each other, and I agreed.

A short while later, I completed my studies and graduated from the Maor Hagola Rabbinical College as a cantor, and I was asked to fill the position as spiritual leader in the town of North Bay, Ontario, a town located about 300 kilometers north of Toronto. It had a population of approximately 35,000 people, including forty Jewish families, many with young children.

The decision was not an easy one. While in Montreal, I had married a survivor of the Holocaust, a woman I had met in DP camp. We had a son, Martin, who was not quite two years old. Should I move my family away from the strong Jewish community in cosmopolitan Montreal to a small town way up north? I approached the rabbi in Montreal for advice.

"Consider the families of North Bay and their precious children," he counseled. "If you don't go and no one else will go, who will teach them *yiddishkeit*, the religious and cultural lessons of Judaism?" My decision was made.

Chapter 12

LIFE GOES ON

When I met with the congregants of the Sons of Jacob Synagogue in North Bay, one of the things I asked them was if they had a *mikvah* (ritual bath). "No, mikvahs are old-fashioned," one of them replied, somewhat surprised at the question. It was more than merely a wish born of nostalgia for my synagogue in Nyíradony. It was an absolute necessity for my wife and me as we observed the laws of family purity as commanded in the Torah. I agreed to their request to serve as their spiritual leader and they, in turn, agreed to build a mikvah at the synagogue.

I was honest with them, telling them that I had by now set my sights on living in the United States. However, I promised to serve them and their community to the very best of my ability until my visa to the United States was approved.

Since arriving in Canada, I had acquired very little knowledge of the English language. In Montreal, I worked and studied with other new arrivals, most of whom spoke only Yiddish. There had been little opportunity or necessity to learn English. Soon after our arrival in North Bay, I realized that I would not be able to fulfill my responsibilities until I mastered this new and difficult language.

I enrolled in an English class in night school. No one in class, except our instructor, Mr. McKee, knew I was Jewish. I always wore a cap, a habit that had remained with me since my youth when I was forced to hide the fact that I was a Jew living among so many anti-Semites.

About five months into the course, Mr. McKee asked each student to prepare a five-minute talk to be given in English in front of the class. When the time came, a young German man was the first to give his speech.

"I don't understand why nearly all of the stores on Main Street are owned by Jews," he began. Mr. McKee caught my eye but kept silent as the speaker continued his thinly veiled tirade against the Jews. This student's English was quite good, and when he finished and sat down, the class applauded him.

The teacher stared directly at me and asked who was going to speak next. I took this cue and went to the front of the room to give my talk. I discarded my prepared outline and began, "I am a Hungarian." I looked directly at the young German. "May I ask where you buy your groceries?"

"At Herman's Supermarket," he replied.

"If you discovered that Ben Herman was a Jew, would you still patronize his store?" I questioned. When he said that he would, I asked him why. He explained that many of his German friends supported themselves by working for Mr. Herman, so of course he would shop there.

"So why are you complaining that most Main Street stores are owned by Jews?" I asked. He looked uncomfortable in his silence.

Then I removed my cap and revealed my yarmulke. "I am a Jew. And because of the Nazis, who thought very much as you do," I declared, "my parents and most of the rest of my family are dead. Murdered."

I asked him his profession. He said he was a farmer. Then I asked him if he was able to make a good living farming. "It is very difficult," he replied. "I barely make enough to survive."

"Then why do you choose farming instead of going to college?" I asked. "You have the opportunity to attend trade school or college just like everyone else. Instead, you and so many others like you are blaming the Jews for their success. The choice of careers is yours, just as it is for the Jews. You must not blame the Jews for your failures just as you must not detract from the Jews for the success that is theirs. They worked for it. They earned it." The young man ran from the classroom and never returned.

The position at the Sons of Jacob Synagogue was my very first job as a full-time spiritual leader, and I threw myself into the work with enthusiasm. I encouraged daily services mornings and evenings, as well as on the Sabbath and Yom Tov. The Talmud Torah Hebrew school and junior congregation began to flourish. I wanted to spread my love of Judaism and knowledge of Torah to all.

While visiting the sick at the hospital one Friday morning, I found that one of the women in my congregation had taken a turn for the worse. Her husband was frantic and pleaded with me to pray to the Almighty on her behalf. He said that I had once mentioned a rabbi in Montreal who was a miracle man.

"There is no such thing as a miracle man," I stressed. "The man to whom I referred is indeed a pious man, but he is not a miracle worker."

"Please say you'll go to him anyway and ask him to pray for my dear wife," the man pleaded. This couple was not observant of the Jewish laws, so I didn't know exactly how to approach the rabbi. Nevertheless, I agreed to go.

When I arrived at the rabbi's home in Montreal, I found a long line of men already waiting to see him. I told his assistant that I must fly home before Sabbath and that my errand was urgent, a matter of life or death. He ushered me into the rabbi's office at once.

After listening to my story, the rabbi wondered aloud how he could approach G-d on this couple's behalf since they had made so little effort to follow His laws. "Perhaps, if they agreed to change, there will be a favorable outcome," he suggested. I phoned the husband from the rabbi's office.

"My dear friend, " I told him, "the rabbi can help you only if you make some commitment toward Torah observance. You could start by promising to light Shabbat candles each Friday evening."

"I cannot answer for my wife, but if she does not light the Shabbat candles, I will," he asserted.

My friend was ecstatic when I met him at the hospital the following Saturday night. His wife was greatly improved, and he cried out with joy, "G-d has answered the rabbi's prayer!" I hastened to explain that it was his commitment to greet the Shabbat with the traditional lighting of the candles that was instrumental in his wife's improvement and not the intervention of prayer by the rabbi. And it was a commitment that he must fulfill from then on.

Although my dreams of living in the United States never diminished, it became necessary for me to acquire Canadian citizenship. The U.S. Immigration Authority, for some inexplicable reason, continued to require that my visa be issued under the Hungarian quota.

Four of my mother's brothers, David, Sam, Ervin, and Sidney, had settled in Gary, Indiana, prior to World War II. Now Dezso and his wife were living there as well. I yearned to be reunited with my family. At long last, our visa came through.

As we said farewell to all the friends we'd made in North Bay over our four years there, the president of the synagogue approached me and asked if I would do him a favor and take the mikvah with us!

In 1960, I moved my family (my wife and my sons, Martin and Jack, who was born in North Bay) to Indiana. Dezso now owned two supermarkets there and offered me a job as manager in the dairy department at his store in Merrilville. I accepted this job for half days only, since I had been hired by Temple Beth El to teach in their Talmud Torah Hebrew school every afternoon. It seemed ever more clear that the Lord had specific plans for me. He was continually steering me toward Jewish education and community service.

In 1962, after thirteen years of marriage, and for reasons too painful to elaborate on, I divorced. Getting a divorce was a most difficult decision for both of us. During that trying time, my mother appeared to me in a dream. She sensed that I was disturbed and encouraged me to share my problem with her. She then directed me to a specific passage in the Torah.

I awoke in the dark of night and hurried to my book to search for the verse. The words my mother suggested made it clear that it was right for me to take action regarding the divorce. In the end, the court awarded me custody of my two children.

It wasn't long before my family and friends began urging me to begin dating again. Frankly, I was not ready, but I could not deny their reasoning. Certainly, for a man in his mid-thirties, a wife and companion would be desirable, as would a mother for the small children. Although not all that enthusiastic, I began to search the personal columns of the *New York Jewish Press* for possible marriage candidates and even corresponded with a few. But nothing clicked. Then a colleague of mine decided to play matchmaker. If he did, I could only hope that he would exercise more caution than I had done when I tried to be a shadchan in the DP camp at Bergen-Belsen.

"Leo, it is not good for a man to be alone," he told me, trying to sound wiser than his years.

"I am not interested in a wife," I insisted. Inside, however, I knew I was not being completely truthful. "What do you have in mind?" I inquired.

He wanted me to meet a young woman named Annette, a widow from the south side of Chicago whom he described as a wonderful person. He rambled on and on, extolling all her lovely qualities to the point that I began to suspect that such a person could not possibly exist.

"Stop!" I demanded. "Tell me something not so wonderful about her."

My friend shook his head. "I really cannot find anything that's not beautiful about this woman. But I must tell you, however, that she has four daughters."

"What? Four daughters? Forget it!" I exclaimed. "How could I possibly support the two of us and her four children plus two of my own? A family of eight? Forget it!"

Still, my friend persisted. "Her children know your children. They attend the same Jewish day school," he told me. My resistance was beginning to crumble. After all, would it really be so bad to meet this person who is already the mother of friends of my children?

"All right, enough already," I told my friend. "See what you can do."

He wasted little time in arranging a double date. He and his wife and I picked up Annette at her home and drove to a theater in downtown Chicago. They tell me the play was *The Tenth Man* by Paddy Chayefsky. I had no idea what was taking place on stage because I was completely preoccupied with staring at this incredibly attractive woman sitting next to me. After the play, we stopped for strawberry ice cream. At the end of the evening, I told Annette that I would call her.

Quite early the next morning, my sister-in-law, Marika, called for my report. Once she learned that I had promised to call Annette, Marika pestered me every day that week until I finally got up enough nerve to do it.

The following Sunday, Annette met me at the South Shore station. I still recall how lovely she appeared to me, wearing a beige hood over her bouffant hairdo. She, too, was in her mid-thirties. Her husband had a congenital heart disease and had died a year before I met her.

She drove me to her home to meet her daughters. Aviva was twelve years old, Renana nine, Miriam almost eight, and Rachel barely two. The little one was a sweet child but a bit unhappy that day as she was suffering from a cold and a runny nose. I have always loved babies, and this one especially touched my heart. They were all extraordinarily special children.

Later, over dinner, we shared our life stories with one another. I wanted Annette to know what kind of person I was. I shared with her every intimate detail of my life — the beautiful childhood times, the horrendous war years, the DP camp, everything. I must admit that I did most of the talking.

Soon we were seeing each other on a regular basis, and I began to feel a growing affection for both Annette and her children. I wanted to take care of them, but I had no idea how we could possibly manage financially. I was also responsible for my sons, Martin, who was then eight years old, and Jack, who was five. On the other hand, I realized that the boys would truly benefit from a mother's care. We both acknowledged that we loved and respected one another, and we even discussed marriage, but the financial concerns kept holding me back.

My mother again came to me in a dream late one night. In this dream, she asked, "What is wrong, my son?"

"*Anyuka*" (mother)," I confided, "I met a wonderful person, but I am afraid to marry her because I will not be able to support eight people.

"Look in the *T'nach* (the Bible), Leizer. There you will find your answer."

When I awoke, I reached for my T'nach and found, "He who takes care of the widow and the orphan will be blessed by G-d." I hurried to the telephone and called Annette. "Will you marry me?"

"Do you know what time it is?!"

"I did not call to ask the time. I asked you if you will you marry me."

"But you are the one who has been so reluctant," she countered.

"Not any more," I said with a smile in my voice.

We were married on December 9, 1962, at the Morrison Hotel in Chicago before family and friends. After a brief honeymoon, we drove back to a the home we had purchased in Gary — a house quite delightfully filled with children.

I was still managing the dairy department in the mornings and teaching in the afternoons and now some evenings as there were so many students in the school that it was necessary for me to teach double sessions.

Our family settled into the roomy, four-bedroom house two blocks from the synagogue where I taught. It was a beautiful life. For the past few years, I had been conducting the High Holiday services for the Jewish community in Iowa City, Iowa. Now the very thought that I would accept such a position out of town on the High Holidays was no longer acceptable to either of us. We very much wanted to be together as a family, especially on the holidays.

The solution was to search for a full-time position as cantor or cantor-teacher. We read the want ads in the *Jewish Post and Opinion* and discovered that Beth Israel Center in Madison, Wisconsin, was in need of a cantor for the coming year. Annette was an alumna of the University of Wisconsin and had spent four years in Madison. She also had family living there. Excited at the prospect, she urged me to apply for the position. An interview was arranged for a Sunday afternoon.

Chapter 13

HAT OF MANY COLORS

My interview before the congregational board of Beth Israel Center in Madison proved successful. I led the *mincha*, the afternoon service, and answered all their inquiries. "Tell us something about your family," one member asked.

I hesitated a moment. "Well, I have been married six months and I have six children."

"Only a cantor could do that!" he exclaimed. I was hired on the spot.

Then came the almost impossible task of finding an affordable house to rent that was large enough for six children and two adults within walking distance of the synagogue. We still owned the house in Gary and couldn't afford to purchase another home until it was sold.

We eventually found a three-bedroom house and moved to Madison in August 1963. The children slept in the bedrooms upstairs while Annette and I turned the living room into a fourth bedroom. Somehow the family made do with one bathroom. Although I could not expect the children (or even my wife for that matter) to understand, I found the whole situation quite luxurious.

As the cantor, I led the services, taught in the Talmud Torah, and served as assistant rabbi to Rabbi Oscar Fleishaker. The rabbinical college in Montreal had granted me *smicha* (ordination as a rabbi), but I did not advertise this fact for I did not want to compete with the rabbi. Besides, I was very content with my position as cantor. We had approximately 200 members, and I devoted myself completely to the work at hand.

I also joined the chaplaincy that served five hospitals. Madison General was the closest, and often my wife and I would spend part of

Shabbat afternoon visiting patients there. Stopping by the nursing homes in the area was also on my weekly schedule.

On January, 27 1966, I took the oath of allegiance to the United States. During the ceremony, Judge Richard Bardwell noticed that I did not utter the last few words: *liberty and justice for all*. When the judge questioned my omission, I replied, "I do not believe that there is either *liberty or justice for all* anywhere, even in this country."

About a year later, I received a few parking tickets for leaving my car in a two-hour parking zone all day Friday and Saturday. When I appeared in court, it Judge Bardwell was presiding. He asked why I had not paid the tickets. I replied that our Sabbath is from sunset to sunset, Friday to Saturday, and that we do not drive either on the Sabbath or on Jewish holidays. I wanted to see if there was justice for all. Indeed there was. I did not have to pay the fine.

During the Vietnam War, there was a great deal of unrest on the University of Wisconsin campus. Students demonstrations, tear gas, and smoke bombs were frighteningly common. In the middle of one night, our house shook ominously. An explosion had rocked the physics lab on campus. Three students who were working there at the time were seriously injured by the bomb.

The next morning, I went to the hospital to visit these students and discovered that one was Jewish. This young man was in serious condition and could not converse. He was surrounded by machines and tubes. I looked in on him often, praying for his recovery.

He had noticed my yarmulke. As soon he could talk, he informed me that he was not interested in religion and, therefore, had no need for a rabbi. I explained, "I am a cantor, not a rabbi."

"I still am not interested," the student replied.

"Okay. Forget about religion," I answered. "Are you interested in talking to another human being?" He said that he was. We visited often and, quite gradually, we began to talk about G-d.

"I am an atheist," the young man declared.

"You are an atheist?" I asked feigning incredulity. "Tell me, what is an atheist?"

"You don't know?" He was genuinely surprised. "An atheist is a person who does not believe in G-d."

"That's fine," I assured him. "Sometimes it is difficult to believe in something you cannot see, but a person who has faith does not have to see G-d. He has G-d in his mind and in his heart." I talked to him about the time I had questioned the existence of G-d when I had watched as my parents and the others sang a prayer to G-d as they were marched into the gas chambers. The young man seemed to take comfort from the fact that I was simply human.

I continued to visit him twice a week during his long months of recuperation. Then one day he exclaimed, "I am going home. I am so happy!"

"What did you say?" I asked.

"I said I am thankful to be going home."

"I am sorry," I said. "Could you tell me once more what you just said?"

He thought for a moment before answering. "I know what you're trying to do. I am thankful that I am going home, but not thankful to G-d."

"Fine, and just whom are you thankful to?"

"No one. I am just thankful."

"Are you really happy you are going home?" I asked.

"Yes," he said firmly.

"Ah, and that is what G-d is." I told him. We remained close friends. Finally, one day he confessed, "I am not an atheist."

"No, you are not," I agreed. "Nobody is an atheist. There is no such person. I am convinced that everyone who says he is an atheist realizes at times that there is some power above who takes care of them, whether they want to admit it or not."

Patients often came to the University Hospital for the treatment of cancer. Shirley, a woman in her early forties from Milwaukee, was one of those. We saw each other often. "Cantor Fettman, I know I am going to die," she told me. "I have but one wish. I would like to see my oldest son become a bar mitzvah."

"You will live to see it happen," I assured her.

The hospital chaplain, Reverend Ehlers, called me early one morning and told me to come to see Shirley as soon as possible. When I entered her room, he told me that she had pulled out the intravenous needles. "What happened to your tubes?" I asked.

"I don't want them anymore. The doctors told me I have only two months to live, and I just want to get it over with."

"Do you believe the doctors?" I questioned.

"I don't know. Really, what choice do I have?" she cried.

"There is another," I whispered to her. "A doctor whom you cannot see but who sees you. You might have faith in Him."

"No, cantor. I'm sorry to say that I don't, not anymore," she said sadly.

I paged the doctor. "Doctor, I understand that you gave Shirley a certain length of time to live." He said that he had. "Are you so sure?" I asked. "You do know that you are playing G-d, don't you?"

He became quite defensive. "Listen here," he admonished me, "we reviewed her case and concluded that she only had a certain amount of time left."

"That's fine," I said. "I am not going to argue with you on the point of whether or not the patient should be told. But please, next time involve a rabbi, a cantor, a priest, or a minister. Perhaps, he or she should be the one to break the news to the patient, or at least be present when you do."

I walked into Shirley's room and told her, "Okay, your doctor told me the same thing he told you. If you believe it, fine. As for me, I don't. Now, what do you want me to do?"

"I have four plots in the Milwaukee Cemetery. Two are for my mother and father, one is for my husband, and the fourth one is for me."

"Shirley," I interrupted, "you will not be buried there."

"What do you mean, I won't be buried there? I paid for the plot. It's all taken care of."

"I understand. But, if you take your own life, you cannot be buried there. You are committing suicide and, therefore, cannot be buried in a Jewish cemetery."

"You are kidding, aren't you?"

"No, I am not."

"Then where will I be buried?"

"You might be buried outside the cemetery. It depends, but in any case, you will not be buried inside the cemetery." I told her gently, but firmly.

"Cantor Fettman, if what you say is true then I want the tubes put back in."

That was February. Shirley returned to her home in Milwaukee a few weeks later, returning every other week to Madison for chemotherapy. Later in the spring, Reverend Ehlers called me to come to see Shirley. A group of doctors crowded around her bed. When I walked into the room, one doctor asked if they should leave. "No," I replied, "You do your thing and I will do mine." I held her hand

and said a prayer, not of last rites, but a prayer for life. She was unconscious. Suddenly, I was aware that one of the doctors was removing the life-support system.

"What are you doing?" I stammered.

"You see what we are doing!" he snapped.

"No, I am not a doctor. I am not sure."

"We're pulling the plug," he said.

"Do you have permission from someone to do this?" I demanded. He said that he did, from her father in Minneapolis. "When did you speak to her father?"

"A few hours ago," came the reply. I asked if I could first make a phone call, and the doctor agreed. I asked him to accompany me while I phoned Shirley's father. It was about 1:00 a.m. when I got him on the phone.

"Mr. Levine, this is Cantor Fettman from Madison. I understand that you gave the doctor permission to kill your daughter."

"What?!" he shouted. "No, no, no! I never did any such thing!" I asked him to tell me what had happened. "The doctors called a few hours ago and told me there was no hope," he explained. "They asked if they could pull the plug."

"Mr. Levine, isn't that the same thing? Pulling the plug might be a nicer term than killing or murdering, but it does boil down to the same thing."

"I had no choice," he said sadly. "I am here, 500 miles away."

"Place your daughter in my hands," I suggested. "Let me take care of her. I am not a doctor, but I can be a surrogate father. The doctor is right here. Would you please tell him that, if he has any questions, he should consult Cantor Fettman?"

As we walked back to the room, the physician asked sarcastically, "Okay, Dr. Fettman, what shall we do now?"

This made me very angry, and I yelled at him. "Don't you dare talk to me like that! I am not a doctor, I am a clergyman. I want you to realize that you are playing with a life. You have to do everything to keep her alive. If someone consulted me earlier, my advice might have been different. Now, however, Shirley is hooked up to a machine and you cannot remove her from it." I phoned my wife to tell her what was going on and that I was going to stay at Shirley's bedside all night. I did not trust the doctors.

About 7:00 a.m., Shirley opened her eyes, surprised to see me there so early in the day. She grasped my hand but, with the tube in her mouth, could not speak. I gave her a pencil and paper. *What are you doing in the hospital so early in the morning?* she wrote.

I answered matter-of-factly, "I came to visit someone and dropped in to see you." Shirley had no idea of what had transpired during the night. At the end of the week, Shirley was discharged from the hospital. She returned every other week to continue treatment. I tried to visit her each time she came to the hospital. When I had not seen her for three or four weeks, I called her home in Milwaukee and Shirley's husband answered the telephone. "How is your wife?' I inquired.

"Don't you know? Shirley died." His voice sounded hollow.

"When?" I stammered. "When did she die?"

"A few weeks before our son's bar mitzvah."

This experience taught me something. If I had permitted her to kill herself or had allowed the doctors to end her life, she would have lost five months of living. I had faith in G-d. The same G-d who had watched over my own bungled attempt at suicide. G-d kept her alive so she could take part in the bar mitzvah plans, even if not the ceremony itself.

I found that others wanted to hear the story of the Holocaust. While I had once delivered a talk in North Bay about my war experiences, it wasn't something I felt I wanted to do on a regular basis. I received an invitation to speak from Reverend Alfred Swan, the pastor of the First Congregational Church in Madison. I had serious reservations about accepting the assignment because the memories of the atrocities were woven inextricably through every fiber of my being. Still, I did not dwell on them. It wasn't so much a matter of trying to forget what had taken place. That was impossible and must never happen. Rather, it was that I was focused on living in the present and planning for the future. I wasn't certain that I wanted to be pulled back into something so abhorrent, so horrifyingly and recently real.

I was also reluctant to accept the pastor's request because of my morbid fear of public speaking. I know that, given my singing before large congregations every week, that it seems odd. Singing is a gift, a talent polished over many years of experience. Public speaking, however, was entirely different. Nonetheless, I agreed.

The pastor went overboard with his campaign to publicize my talk. When the day arrived, I found myself standing in the elevated pulpit of the First Congregational Church staring down into the faces of several hundred people. That was the last time I saw their eyes. I glanced down at my papers and began to talk, and never once looked up.

When I finished, someone in the audience asked if he could have a copy of my presentation. Somewhat sheepishly, I held up the papers and showed everyone that they were blank. At that time, I could not force myself to put my experiences down on paper. Somehow, doing so would have made the memories even more permanent than they already were. I chose instead to speak from the heart as I recounted my life in Hungary and in the concentration and labor camps.

It hit me that the reason I could not look at the audience was not solely because of my fear of public speaking. It was also due to misplaced blame. I couldn't look at them because they had been safe and sound in the United States while my family was being tortured and murdered. I felt, and still do, that if the countries of the free world had spoken up and taken action against Hitler when his evil designs were first known, millions of lives could have been spared. Standing before this congregation, these poor souls represented the free world to me. I held them somehow responsible for the genocide of the Third Reich.

One day, I was interviewed on a radio talk show. I spoke about my experiences in the concentration camps. The radio audience called in questions, which I answered to the best of my ability.

"Cantor Fettman," one woman caller said. "I am of German origin. I would like to know why we are constantly being reminded of what the Nazis did more than twenty years ago." I thought for a moment and gave her a firm answer. When I returned home, my wife asked why I had not answered that woman.

"But I did answer her," I insisted.

Later, when I stopped at the synagogue, Rabbi Fleishaker confronted me with the same question. Then the telephone rang and Reverend Swan of the First Congregational Church also asked me. When I explained that the show's host had apparently deleted my answer without my knowledge, Reverend Swan invited me to answer the question after his sermon the following Sunday morning, and I accepted.

There was an overflow of congregants at the church. After his sermon, Reverend Swan repeated the question this woman had asked me on the air: "Cantor Fettman, I am of German origin. Why are we being constantly reminded of what the Nazis did more than twenty years ago?"

I repeated what I had said during the radio program. "I am going to answer your question with a question. Why are we Jews constantly reminded of a crime that we never committed that took place two thousand years ago?" The applause filled the sanctuary.

We then had an informal question-and-answer period during which someone in the audience asked, "Are you a kike, Cantor?"

I was not familiar with the word, so I leaned over to Reverend Swan and asked him what the word meant. He explained that it was a derogatory name for a Jew. Then I looked at the man who had posed the question. "Yes, I am a kike. And, for that matter, you worship a kike!" He sat down without saying another word.

A few weeks later, this same man phoned me and asked if I would meet with him, and I agreed. When we were once again face to face, he said "Cantor Fettman, I need your help. I want you to convert me!"

I looked at him and said, "What? You want to become a kike? What made you change?"

"After you told me that I worshiped a kike, I began to read up on the Jewish faith. I've really learned a lot. I had no idea how much your people have suffered! I really want to help the Jews."

"You really want to help the Jews?"

"Yes, I do."

I told him, "Then I'll give you an easier way. Be a good Christian!"

Abe Rosenberg and his dear wife, Celia, became very close friends of ours. He was my mentor, and they were almost like parents to us. Abe suffered from emphysema and, in time, became quite ill. I visited him often during the many weeks he was hospitalized.

A strange feeling came over me one Shabbat morning just before I was to begin chanting my portion of the service. Somehow I knew instinctively that I must go see Abe at the hospital immediately. Rabbi Fleishaker had moved from Madison and was replaced by a rabbi who was not quite as easy to get along with. I leaned over to him and said softly, "Rabbi, I am sorry, but I have to go to the hospital to see Mr. Rosenberg."

"You can't leave in the middle of the service!" he exclaimed.

"Rabbi, I truly am very sorry, but I must."

The hospital was located about five blocks from the synagogue. I raced down the street and into his room and stood just inside the doorway. He had lapsed into a coma. One of the several doctors surrounding his bed noticed me and asked what I wanted.

"I came to see Mr. Rosenberg. I would like to say a prayer, if I may." I took Abe's hand in mine while the doctors continued to work on him. Suddenly, he looked up at me and questioned, "How did you get here?"

"What do you mean, how did I get here?"

"It's Shabbat," he answered. "Did you walk?"

"Yes, I did," I told him. The doctor looked on in amazement as we spoke. They told me to keep conversing with him. After about five minutes, he stopped talking, but we continued to communicate with our eyes.

Afterwards, I returned to the synagogue. The rabbi was upset with what I had done. At this point, however, I really did not care. I did what I knew I had to do. When Shabbat ended, I drove back to the hospital. Celia Rosenberg and the family were there. They told me that Abe had died that afternoon.

"We heard that he was talking to you," they said.

"Yes, he was," I told them. As we were speaking, the rabbi walked in. He looked at me rather sternly and ordered, "Cantor Fettman, since I am here now, you can go home." I stood up and prepared to leave.

"You are not going anywhere," Gil Rosenberg interjected. "We want you to stay here." He turned to the rabbi and said, "You may go home." Later, the rabbi and I had a not-so-friendly talk. I was angry at his pettiness over such an important issue and banged on his table. I believe I may have cracked it.

❖❖❖

WHAT'S IN A NAME?

Samuel Kulakowski was one of our regular daily worshipers. One morning after service, he asked me a favor. "Would you be so kind as to accompany me to court next Monday? I am going to change my name."

Mr. Kulakowski was a sincere man and a good friend, much older than I. He had been born in the old country and could barely speak English. I was honored to be able to help him.

When Monday arrived, I drove over to his house. As we got in my car to head downtown, his wife, Esther, waved from the window. He was in a jovial mood as we pulled into the parking lot at the courthouse. A few minutes later, we both stood in the judge's chamber. Judge Middlestat smiled down at us.

"So, Mr. Kulakowski, you are petitioning the court to change your name. What changes would you like to make?"

"Sam! Sam!" he shouted with a grin. "I want to be called Sam Kulakowski." The judge and I looked at each other in shocked disbelief.

❖❖❖

Hoping to advance my position, I answered an ad for a cantorial position in Omaha, Nebraska. At the time, I did not know where in the world Omaha was located. The year was 1973, and my Madison synagogue was starting to lean from Orthodox toward Conservative Judaism. Because of the nature of my faith, it was essential for me to serve an Orthodox congregation.

Within a few weeks, I received a reply that the position had already been filled. However, the committee wrote, it would keep my letter on file. A year later, Dr. Haskell Morris called from Omaha quite unexpectedly. He identified himself as chairman of the cantor's search committee for Beth Israel Synagogue and explained, "Cantor Fettman, some time ago you applied for the position of cantor. If you are still interested, we would like to invite you for an interview."

I was excited about the opportunity, but I wanted to know the age of the rabbi. I found that it is easier to work with someone close to my age, and so I asked, "Dr. Morris, tell me, how old is your rabbi?"

"Why don't you ask him yourself," he answered. "He's on the line." I was too flustered to talk, but fortunately the rabbi spoke first.

"How young do you want me to be?" came Rabbi Nadoff's voice over the line. I told him my age, and he said, "I believe there is a three-year difference between our ages. Do you think that will pose a problem?" I could hear the smile in his voice. I went to Omaha for the interview.

Chapter 14

Nebraska – The Good Life

Under the spiritual leadership of Rabbi Isaac Nadoff, the Beth Israel Synagogue in Omaha was a vibrant congregation of 700 families. The main sanctuary, which seated about 400 worshipers, was impressive, and a new Jewish Community Center was nearing completion on the west side of the city across the road from Boys Town.

I flew in for a Sabbath and was the guest of the rabbi and his wife. I was invited to participate in a meeting of the synagogue's Board of Education. "Is your school a Hebrew school or a Talmud Torah?" I inquired of them. The members asked whether there was a difference.

"Definitely," I answered. "What is your goal? Is it to teach Hebrew, or to teach the words of Torah, Jewish law, and Jewish observance and ethics?"

"We are a Talmud Torah!" was the unanimous reply.

The interview was a success, and although the committee offered me a contract, I put off signing it until my wife could visit and give her approval. She did, and we moved to Omaha at the end of the summer in 1974. On the bridge over the Missouri River, we were welcomed by a sign which read "Nebraska — the Good Life." Our family was now half the size, as just our two sons and youngest daughter were still at home. The others were already out on their own.

My commitment to Jewish education has always been very strong. I wanted to make a positive impact on my students as well as their parents. I developed programs that involved the parents' participation. As soon as we arrived, I began instructing two young men for their b'nai mitzvah. Jewish education was of utmost importance to me. Sadly, however, it appeared that it evolved around preparation for a performance at the bar or bat mitzvah. Once that ceremony had taken place, there appeared to be little interest in continuing the study of Judaism. I felt that perhaps if my fellow congregants had endured the anti-Semitism of Europe, they would not take their religious freedom so much for granted.

Wanting to place further emphasis on adult education, I began classes in basic Hebrew, Jewish holidays, and Jewish life in general. Several men were eager to learn the cantillation, the chanting of liturgical texts from the Torah and the Haftorah. Rabbi Nadoff also assigned me to teach a class for those who intended to marry into the Jewish faith and wanted to convert to Judaism. I insisted that the students' Jewish partners also attend class. The results were amazing. The converted Jews made excellent students, and their enthusiasm was contagious. Their partners born into the Jewish faith had never approached their Judaism on an adult level, and what they learned made a tremendous impact on them.

"The Good Life" of Nebraska was at first elusive. My wife experienced some difficulty adjusting to the move, and during our first winter in Omaha, she underwent major surgery. Just a couple of months later, I had some polyps removed from my vocal cords. Slowly, things improved and we came to embrace our new life and our new home.

When Annette and I realized that we were going to stay in Omaha, we began looking for a permanent place to live. There was a house that I had admired while walking through the neighborhood. It was on the corner of 57th Street and Hamilton. As I thought about the house, I experienced an unsettling flashback to my childhood. Strangely, I did not think I could be comfortable living on a corner. As in Nyíradony, I felt a need for the security of living in the middle of the block with houses on either side. It's hard to explain. Still the house attracted me whenever we went on our Sabbath walks. When my neighbor told me that he was planning to put it up for sale in the near future, we agreed to buy it, and, in April 1976, moved into our new home.

I must confess, I never became accustomed to living on the corner. I loved the house, but I had a nightly ritual (and still do) of closing all the blinds and double-locking all the doors. On Chanukah, our menorah is not displayed in the window as is traditionally done. Ironically, it is supposed to be a sign to all of religious freedom. Old habits and fears die hard.

In addition to education, my position at Beth Israel Synagogue as cantor-teacher and rabbi's assistant included a wide variety of tasks. I visited hospital patients and the elderly and kept in touch with our home-bound congregants. Kosher supervision was another responsibility, both in Omaha and in other regions of the state. My wife supervised the kashruth at the Jewish Community Center and then the Rose Blumkin Home for the elderly when it was constructed on the same campus. And there were the Israel Bond dinners and endless meetings of various synagogue committees. Our schedules were quite full and our lives enormously happy. Still, I did not feel that I was fulfilling G-d's mission for me. Indeed, I struggled long and hard even to figure out what it was. Eventually, I was led in the right direction.

I came across a book titled *The Hoax of the Twentieth Century*, written by Professor Arthur R. Butz of Northwestern University and published in 1977. Butz seems to be in the forefront of those would have you believe that the Holocaust either never occurred, or has been greatly exaggerated. I couldn't believe my eyes! How dare they suggest that what I had witnessed, what I had endured, and what I had lost were not real, but only the invention of some so-called Jewish conspiracy to engender support for Judaic causes. I was outraged! But I will credit his book with one thing — from that moment on, I was fully aware of the mission that G-d had in mind for me. I knew I must dedicate the balance of my life to teaching others about the horrible reality of the Holocaust while conveying a message that the answer for the future lies in love and understanding.

A short while later, a Mr. Lyle Reed phoned. "I teach social studies at Millard South High School," he explained. "Would you come speak about your experiences during the Holocaust?" We made an appointment for my talk. Although I had spoken on the subject in North Bay and in Madison, this marked the real beginning of my role as a Holocaust speaker. I delivered my message to the students, and they listened with rapt attention. I returned every year for the next seventeen years to speak before Mr. Reed's classes. The following is an excerpt from a letter that he wrote at the time of his retirement and that was published in the *Jewish Press*:

> My students and I are so very much grateful to him
> for his dedication to young people. Over the past seventeen

years, Cantor Fettman has spoken to over 6,000 of my pupils. They have related to me that he has had a profound positive influence on them. With bigotry and hatred running rampant in the United States against certain groups of people, I strongly feel that every high school student needs to have a "Cantor Fettman" address them. It is of extreme importance to enlighten our young people to eliminate these dreadful components of our society.

Each year, the number of requests for me to speak grew steadily. I began to fulfill my goal to educate the public about this sad period in our recent history and to encourage brotherhood and understanding between all peoples.

Through these speaking engagements, my wife and I have met many fascinating people. One invitation came from Mount Marty College in Yankton, South Dakota, where we were treated royally and even slept in the bishop's quarters. The church was exquisite, and my talk, arranged through the Jewish Chatauqua Society, seemed well received.

Another interesting assignment was during the visit to Billings, Montana, where I was to lecture at Eastern Montana College and Rocky Mountain College. Also, I was surprised to be asked to speak to the homeless at the local Rescue Mission while I was in town. These bereft souls were no strangers to degradation. I explained to those gathered in the mission's prayer hall how the Nazis had called me "dog," how I had lost hope and had tried to commit suicide, and how still I survived and regained my self respect. Much to my surprise, shouts of "amen" came from the audience. I left the mission with tears in my eyes.

Over a period of years, one Montana bigot had been writing to *The Billings Gazette*. His letters carried only one theme — that the Holocaust had never occurred, that it was a concoction of Jewish imagination in attempt to win sympathy. The newspaper had printed his letters without comment. On November 8, 1989, the day of my talk, however, *The Billings Gazette* published the following editorial:

Holocaust Undeniable

The denials come like shrieks on a winter wind.

The Holocaust was a fabrication, a conspiracy to convince the Allies that European Jews deserved a homeland, deserved Israel.

Six million Jews were not killed in those dark days, told to take "showers" of poisonous gas, Nazi scavengers roaming through the bodies, stripping gold teeth from silent mouths, cutting wedding rings from dead fingers.

The Nazis didn't kill children, didn't stack bodies like cordwood in crematoriums, turning human flesh into heavy, black smoke and ash.

But the denials have no more substance than the shrieks of those winter winds. We know better.

We are haunted by newsreels of Allied troops opening the gates of concentration camps, greeted by wide eyes staring from skeletal bodies in steel cages.

We wonder how it could have happened. How one of the world's most civilized nations could have been set on such a barbaric, evil course by one megalomaniac's vision.

We fear that the seeds of that insanity lie in all of us, awaiting cultivation by still another madman.

And we wonder at the denials.

Is the truth so terrible that we cannot bear it, that to accept the truth is to accept the darkness that dwells within each of us?

And that's the root of it, that terrible question: How we would have reacted if we had been in a nation suddenly driven mad?

And we answer that question each time we listen without protest to neo-Nazis talk of the conspiracy of the "International Jewry." Each time, our silence sets another concentration camp post in the ground.

Listen to a victim of the Holocaust at 7:30 tonight at Congregation Beth Aaron.... All those denials are empty as the wind.

With the goal of improving relations between Jews and non-Jews, our Beth Israel Sisterhood sponsored a "Know Thy Neighbor Sabbath" every year during Brotherhood Month. Invitations were extended to every church in the area and hundreds of people would crowd our sanctuary. There appeared to be a great interest in our faith. After the services, I was asked many questions about Judaism, our faith, and our traditions.

Speaking wherever and whenever I can has become a major occupation of my life. While some speaking assignments have come through the Anti-Defamation League, the vast majority have come through referrals. I have spoken to audiences of all ages. I have spoken at public and church schools, colleges and universities, service clubs, and many other organizations.

On one of my lecture tours, I spoke at a school in Calloway, Nebraska (population 596). The mayor of the town told me that the town had been founded by the Ku Klux Klan. Indeed, he added, there was a bronze plaque in the town's little museum attesting to this fact. A chest, however, had been moved in front of the plaque to hide its ignoble message. I had spoken before much larger audiences; however, I had a great sense of satisfaction in delivering in a town of Ku Klux Klan heritage my message advocating love and understanding among all people.

On another occasion, I expected to address 200 to 300 young people at Southeast High School in Lincoln, Nebraska. When it was time for my introduction, I was ushered into a large auditorium filled to overflowing with 1,800 students and about 125 faculty members! This was the largest audience I'd ever had. The principal turned to me saying, "I am not certain how to get them quiet."

"Don't worry," I assured him. "Let me do it." I took the microphone and began chanting loudly in Hebrew. There was dead silence. I then spoke for about an hour and then opened the floor for questions.

One young woman asked whether I could find justification for the experiments conducted by the Nazis. What if it were found, she wanted to know, that medical science had actually been advanced by these experiments?

"I don't think that there has been any proof that mankind has gained any benefit whatsoever from these sadistic tests," I replied. "But let us say hypothetically that something positive *was* derived. Would you volunteer your mother for such an experiment?"

"Oh, no, no! Not my mother!" she shouted, pale and stunned at the very thought of it.

I asked, "It's okay, my mother but not your mother?"

One morning when Rabbi Nadoff and I were drinking coffee in his office, we discussed retirement. "Are you planning to retire when you reach sixty-five?" I inquired.

"Why do you ask? Do you want to get rid of me?"

"Why should I?" I asked, telling him that I presumed most people retire when they reach the age of sixty-five.

"Look," he explained, "I will no doubt always be teaching and sermonizing and comforting the sick. I might as well get paid for it!"

Soon after our talk, the rabbi became ill and was incapacitated for many weeks. I took over his responsibilities while continuing to teach classes and lead services. I thought all along that he would recover within a few months, but this was not to be.

One morning, I visited the rabbi in the hospital. He motioned to his bedside and said in a weak voice, "I was wrong. I now know I won't be able to do all the things I planned for the future. No more traveling, no anything." His voice was trembling. I instantly decided to retire when I turned sixty-five the next year. I surprised my wife with this declaration as soon as I came in the door.

As the weeks passed, it became obvious that the rabbi would not be able to resume his duties. I knew in my heart that I would do all I could to help keep the synagogue strong. I would continue to carry the double workload until a new rabbi was found to lead Beth Israel Synagogue.

I informed the congregation president of my intention to retire at age sixty-five, quickly adding that I would be available to assist the synagogue as long as needed. In the meantime, a new cantor was hired, and I was relieved of my teaching duties. I continued to function as rabbi, giving sermons and conducting funerals and unveilings (the dedication of a headstone at the grave of a loved one). Sadly, there were too many of these.

In April 1983, Annette and I attended a gathering of Holocaust survivors in Washington, D.C. I searched in vain for Sandor or even any information about him. I admit that I still held out hope that, by some miracle, he was still alive and had just been unable to find me.

While we were there, however, I did meet the daughter of a survivor who was with Margit in the ghetto. She said that she understood that Margit's little daughter Leah had been injured in Nyirmihalydi and could not walk very well. Or perhaps she was ill;

she wasn't certain. Regardless of the circumstances, the hospital in Nyirmihalydi had turned them away because they were Jewish. This woman's mother was Margit's neighbor, and she said that Margit had been forced to spend several days in the synagogue in their town, as we had in ours. This woman helped Margit while in the synagogue and in the ghetto. That was all she knew.

In 1984, we traveled to Jerusalem to visit our children who were living there and to join in a gathering of Hungarian survivors of the Holocaust. Again, I allowed myself to hope for some sign of Sandor. It was not to be.

The meeting was held at Binyane Uma Auditorium. Each room was designated by a Hungarian state and county. We went to the rooms labeled Szabolcs Megye (the name of the state in which Nyíradony is located) and Hajdu (where Debrecen is located). Before the program, one person asked me who I was and where I had lived. I told him I was Hungarian, born and raised in Nyíradony, and had gone to Debrecen to study and work.

"Did you know Cantor Friedlander?" he asked.

"Yes," I said. "I conducted the service at his synagogue on the second day of Rosh Hashanah. At the age of fifteen, I joined his choir."

"Do you know where he is?" he asked.

"No," I said shrugging my shoulders.

"There he is," he said, pointing to an elderly man. As I looked, I could not believe my eyes. Was it really him? I walked over to him and asked whether he was actually Cantor Friedlander.

"Yes, I am. Who are you?"

"I am Leo Fettman from Omaha, Nebraska, in America. I joined the choir in your synagogue. I conducted the service during Rosh Hashanah when you had laryngitis."

Although he did not recall the incident, he welcomed me and asked, "Do you remember the rabbi, Dr. Weisz Pal?"

"Yes, Rabbi Weisz Pal," I replied. "Where is he?"

"Here he is," he said as he put his arm around the man standing next to him.

"Are you Dr. Rabbi Weisz Pal?" I asked with amazement.

"I am Dr. Rabbi Weisz Pal, and he is Friedlander," he replied. "I am still a rabbi working for the Israeli government. Cantor Friedlander, however, is no longer an active cantor. Therefore, he is Friedlander only," he added jokingly.

"Are you a cantor in America?" Cantor Friedlander asked me. "Yes, in Nebraska."

Cantor Friedlander asked me to chant *Kel Maley Rachamim*, the memorial prayer at the service to commemorate the Hungarian Jews who had perished in concentration camps, the same prayer I had sung aboard the freighter on the way to Montreal. "Yes," I said, "but on one condition — that you will also chant something." Cantor Friedlander agreed. It seemed like *déjà vu*, just as when he asked me to conduct the Rosh Hashanah service so many years before in Debrecen.

Later that day, he announced to the audience, "I introduce to you the chief cantor of Omaha, Nebraska!" As I chanted the prayer, I recalled the excitement I had felt as a young man conducting that Rosh Hashanah service in his synagogue. G-d seemed to be smiling upon us. Then, Cantor Friedlander chanted a psalm. When he opened his mouth, the sound he intoned was so rich and powerful. He still possessed a voice I wish I had now.

Back in the United States, the rabbi search committee had engaged a new rabbi. Three cantors sang together for Rabbi Nadoff's tribute dinner and also were invited to sing as part of the musical tribute at my retirement dinner in March 1992.

The event honored Annette and me upon the completion of our eighteenth year of serving Beth Israel Synagogue. There were several presentations and speeches, but what made the evening personally special was that our grandson, Yoni, spoke on behalf of our family. He was only fifteen years old at the time but spoke as a mature adult. Rabbi Nadoff recovered enough to deliver a tribute. In part, he said:

> Cantor and I often talked and I remember us saying to each other, "teaching is like planting seeds." The results are not immediately evident. In time the fruit appears…and how sweet the fruit will be. And a second factor, a very determining factor in the aspect of his life is the fact that he is, as you know, a survivor of the Holocaust. He was recalled to life, and survival thrust upon him a mission, a mission to tell and retell the events surrounding the Holocaust. And, as we say in the *Haggaddah* as we sit around the Passover table when we speak about the persecution of the Jewish people when they were in Egyptian bondage, the more we tell and retell, the more praiseworthy we are, and so the cantor too.

And so he speaks all over the city and all over the state, college students, high school and elementary students, teacher conferences, there is no end to the audiences he addresses. He is their teacher about the Holocaust, reminding them about the evils of bigotry and hatred and prejudices and anti-Semitism, the evils that led to the Holocaust, the Shoah. The evils that led to the horrors of the concentration camps. For most of them, this was their first and perhaps the only introduction to the subject of the Holocaust. And his impact on them is powerful and lasting. And he influenced many lives and left a mark on many individual lives, talking about the Holocaust so many years after the fact. If you will ask, is this important? The answer is, it is most important. Fewer and fewer living witnesses remain. In the passage of time, there is the danger that there will be no more calls to tell the tale of the Holocaust. Already throughout the world, you have read of this, you have heard of this. Throughout the world there is a conspiracy to dismiss the Holocaust, to deny that it occurred.

They call it a myth, a vastly overblown event. Even one of our presidential candidates, Pat Buchanan, is referring to the Holocaust as an exaggeration on the part of the Jewish people.

There is a movement of Holocaust revisionists. That is why it is important to teach the world about the Holocaust and remind the world about the Holocaust.... We must tell the truth about the Holocaust to counteract the revisionists to overcome the indifference and to prevent amnesia from setting in.

Eventually, it was my turn to respond to all these accolades and my comments were to be followed by a musical tribute. I spoke for about fifteen minutes and then uttered my closing words, "G-d, where are You?" At that moment, all the lights went out, and all 400 people sat in complete darkness! We were informed that a car had hit a transformer, shutting off power to a large section of mid-town Omaha.

The cast had rehearsed for months. The show, however, could not go on without lights or a sound system. My attitude was that two parties are always better than one. And so, in April, a second party was held. The long-awaited musical tribute to my wife and me was performed at the synagogue. Just to make sure they were prepared this time, the cast marched in carrying flashlights.

Rabbi Nadoff could not join us for the second party. He had been hospitalized once again, and this time there was no remission. Within a couple of weeks, he was gone. This was a great loss for myself, Beth Israel, and the entire community. His tribute to me was his very last public address.

Since my retirement, I have retired on several other occasions as well. I keep being called here and there to serve. When I finish an assignment, I retire once again. One of my commitments was to serve as the cantor for the Jewish High Holidays at a synagogue in Hawaii. A tough assignment, but if someone had to do it, it might as well have been me!

For each of three years, I spent at least two weeks in Kailua-Kona on the island of Hawaii, where I also taught both children and adults. The congregation consisted of only seventy or eighty people, and they really didn't have a formal synagogue. Instead, they met in a local hotel. Through telephone calls, tape recordings, and faxes, I even trained two of their young boys for their bar mitzvah. I also helped them establish a Jewish cemetery.

One of the most rewarding aspects of my professional life, however, is being able to speak about my experiences during the Holocaust and to translate those ordeals into a message of hope and love for people everywhere. I believe I most enjoy those opportunities where I can speak and, hopefully, enlighten, non-Jewish audiences.

In 1995, I was interviewed by the Survivors of the Shoah Visual History Foundation. The foundation was established by Steven Spielberg at about the time his movie *Schindler's List* was released. The group's purpose is to record as many survivors' stories as possible. They recognize, as we all must, that the generation of survivors is aging. Soon, the story will no longer be able to be told by our lips alone. That is, until Mr. Spielberg decided to videotape our stories for posterity. More than 45,000 such stories have been recorded. In February 1996, I received a letter from Mr. Spielberg, in which he said:

> Dear Mr. Fettman:
> In sharing your personal testimony as a survivor of the Holocaust, you have granted future generations the opportunity to experience a personal connection with history.

Your interview will be carefully preserved as an important part of the most comprehensive library of testimonies ever collected. Far into the future, people will be able to see a face, hear a voice, and observe a life, so that they may listen and learn, and always remember...."

All my best,
Steven Spielberg

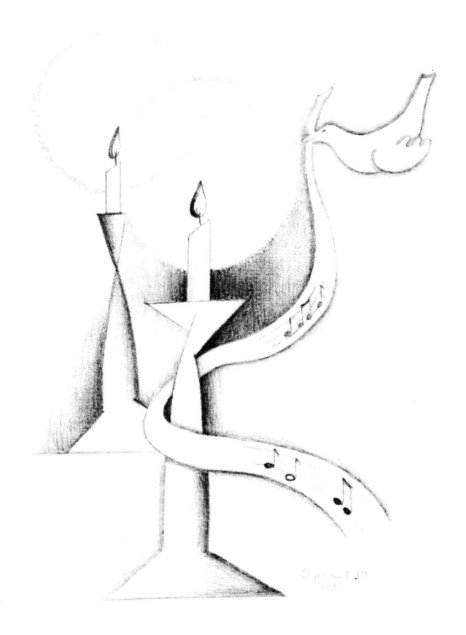

PART THREE

Chapter 15

No Forgetting. . .No Forgiving

B efore I speak to school groups, I require that the students read about the Holocaust and about Judaism. I am not there to entertain them. I am a teacher. I want them to learn even before my arrival.

I have been asked many interesting (and sometimes painful) questions during my presentations at these schools and elsewhere. I believe and hope that these questions and my answers have been helpful and healing for my audiences. I know they have been for me. I would like to share a few of these with you:

How can you smile while you relive your terrible story?

Humor helped keep me alive in the camps. I have always tried to find a reason to smile in everything I have done. A task obviously far more difficult at some times than at other. Now, when I share my horrible experiences with an audience, I smile and add some humor. If I allowed my inner feelings of anger and resentment to show, no one would listen to me. With some humor and a smile, hopefully my message will come across to my listeners.

Cantor Fettman, how are your feelings toward the German people today?

You really have to be more specific in your question. You ask me how my feelings are toward the German people or toward the Nazis? There's a difference. Maybe at the time of the war I didn't feel it, but there is a big difference. During and immediately after the war, many labeled all Germans as Nazis. That's the same as if I robbed a bank and it was reported that a Jew had committed the crime.

So I get quite upset when people say that all Germans were Nazis. That's simply not true. But let me add, the way I felt toward the Nazis at that time was the same as I felt toward the Americans. That's a very strong statement. What am I saying? America is a free country. Why didn't they do something? Why didn't they blow up the tracks at Auschwitz and many other places? They didn't. Of course, I'm not speaking about the American people. I am speaking of the American government. They had opportunities to help the Jews and the others who were falling victim to Hitler's madness, and they didn't act. They are guilty of murder.

Why did you begin speaking publicly about the Holocaust?

When I first read about the Holocaust deniers, I became very upset and knew I had to speak out. Having experienced firsthand the atrocities of the Nazis, I realized it was my responsibility to tell the truth.

Did you share your experiences with your children?

Yes, I did tell my children about them. At first, they were too young to comprehend. As they grew older, though, they became angry that the free world was so silent for so long. They, in turn, are now speaking to groups about the Holocaust.

How could you maintain your sanity during the Holocaust?

It was quite difficult to do so. At times, I questioned if I was being successful. But I knew that if I wanted to stay alive, a strong will and a strong mind were necessary. It is amazing what you can do to survive against incredible odds. Through strong desire and strong faith, almost anything is possible.

Were you on Schindler's list?

No, I was not. I did see the movie but felt it spared the audience the true horrors of the camps. Director Steven Spielberg was aware that the public could not appreciate a full account of the atrocities. There are, however, important lessons in the movie: A person can change, and one person can make a difference! We all have the ability to change, and we all have the opportunity to make a difference and make this world a better place for everyone.

Why were people moved from camp to camp?

The Nazis did not want us to know exactly what they were doing or what they were building. We never once completed a project that we had started. Instead, we were moved to another camp and another project. It was like that throughout the war.

Have you ever gone back to Europe and visited any of the camps you were in?

No. I still am not ready to go back. Perhaps I never will be. I could not do so without being overwhelmed by the fact that innocent people were murdered there. To me, much of Europe is still soaked with the blood of those who died so needlessly.

Can you forgive the Nazis? Can you forget what they did?

Forget? Never. I am not permitted to forget it. And neither must you. Can I forgive the Nazis? More than fifty years have passed, and so far I cannot. Maybe the time will come to forgive them, perhaps tomorrow. But if I do forgive them, I can forgive them only for what they did to me. I have no right whatsoever to forgive the Nazis for what they did to my parents. If you hurt a person, you must ask forgiveness from the person you have injured. In other words, no forgetting and no forgiving.

How did you feel about your religion after what you had seen and gone through?

I think I remained as religious as I was before, and I think I have become a better human being. It was not easy, however. When I arrived in Montreal, I was still quite troubled by the fact that I had survived and my parents and family had not. I visited with a rabbi and told him of the problems I was having. "Why am I alive and my parents are not?" I asked him. "Is it because I am a better Jew?" I added facetiously. He looked at me and smiled. "Your parents fulfilled their mission on earth. You have not. That's why you're still alive."

Calling on my humor developed in the dark days and nights of the concentration camp, I said to him, "You know what, Rabbi? I'm going to work very slowly to fulfill my mission!"

Cantor Fettman, how could you with any conscience place the bodies of your fellow Jews into the ovens of the crematorium?

Before I answer your question, I'd like all of you to do something for me. (There were about 400 people in the auditorium, and I asked them all to stand, and they did.) Place your arms over your head and turn slowly all the way around. (They did.) Now, I'd like you turn around in the opposite direction. (And they did.) Now please be seated. There are several hundred of you. I am just one person, a Jew, and an old one at that. I don't have a machine gun, a club, or a large snarling dog. I have nothing, yet you obeyed me. Consider the consequences of the differences. That is my answer.

Chapter 16

"Hitler" Is Alive And Well

H itler is alive and well. I do not like saying that, but it is always at the back of my mind. The Holocaust can happen again if we permit it, and unless we speak out, we are doing just that. We cannot afford to be silent. "Am I my brother's keeper?" you ask. My answer is a resounding, "Yes, I am!" We all are. We are all brothers and sisters who must care for each other. It is incumbent upon each of us not to remain silent in the face of bigotry and hatred whenever and wherever we encounter them.

Those Who Deny History

When I first read *The Hoax of the Twentieth Century: The Case Against the Presumed Extermination of European Jewry* by Arthur R. Butz, I was outraged. Butz claims the Holocaust was an exaggerated story concocted by Jews for public-relations purposes. It simply could not have happened, he said. But then I figured, what harm can just one book do? Sadly, I learned, it was not just one book. There are many people who have dedicated their lives to denying the facts surrounding the deaths of millions of innocent people at the hands of the Nazis.

There are some who say we should not argue with those who attempt to revise the history of the Holocaust. To do so, they suggest, only gives them more credibility. Others say we must confront them at every opportunity. I must admit that I was uncertain at the beginning. As I began speaking publicly about the Holocaust, however, I no longer doubted the importance of teaching the truth. Looking into the young faces in my audience, children of parents even too young to remember the war, I realized the important link to history that I and other survivors represent.

What is the effect of the Holocaust revisionists? What price do we pay by remaining silent? Should schools continue to teach about the Holocaust? In my opinion, a survey conducted in 1993 when the Holocaust Memorial Museum opened in Washington, D.C., answered these questions. The poll asked, "Do you think it possible or impossible that the Holocaust did not happen? A shocking twenty-two percent of adults and twenty percent of high school students in the United States said they believe it is possible that the Holocaust never occurred.

I read that a 1998 poll commissioned by the museum revealed that one out of five Americans is not aware that Jews were killed in the Holocaust. On a more positive note, though, the survey also showed that eighty percent of the people polled placed the Holocaust just behind the American Revolution as one of history's most important lessons, and six out of ten wanted to know more about the Holocaust.

Still, should we really care about the deniers and revisionists? Aren't they simply harmless members of lunatic fringe groups operating outside the mainstream of society and of no danger to anyone but themselves? Perhaps in the beginning that was true. Few were even aware of the claims and fewer still found them credible. Somewhere along the way, things began to change.

Butz is an associate professor of electrical and computer engineering at Northwestern University. On May 13, 1991, he wrote an article titled "A Short Introduction to the Study of Holocaust Revisionism" that was published in the school's newspaper, *The Daily Northwestern*. His stature as a professor at a prestigious university seemed to lend an air of respectability to the whole messy affair of rewriting history. That he is in a position, as a teacher, to influence the minds of young adults, is even more serious.

In *The Daily Northwestern* article, Butz wrote:

> I see three principal reasons for the widespread but erroneous belief in the legend of millions of Jews killed by the Germans during World War II: U.S. and British troops found horrible piles of corpses in the west German camps they captured in 1945 (*e.g.*, Dachau and Belsen), there are no longer large communities of Jews in Poland, and historians generally support the legend.

I will do my best to contain my anger as I repeat for you his explanations. The Nazis' "Final Solution," he said, was merely a program of evacuation, resettlement, and deportation and had nothing whatsoever to do with extermination. He claimed typhoid was responsible for the deaths of millions, and that the shaving of hair and the showers and the Zyklon B gas and the crematoria were all humanitarian efforts by the Germans to control the disease. When the Nazi organization began to collapse near the end of the war, Butz said, such efforts ceased, and disease became rampant throughout all of the camps. He alleged that the decline in Europe's post-war Jewish population is attributable to the massive immigration of Jews to Palestine, the United States, and other countries.

Finally, he stated that the evidence offered in the Nuremberg trials after the war was "almost all oral testimony and 'confessions.' I am not arguing," Butz wrote, "that the trials were illegal or unfair; I am arguing that such historical logic as the legend rests on must not be countenanced. Such events cannot happen without generating commensurate and contemporaneous evidence for their reality.... One may as well believe that New York City was burned down, if confessions to the deed can be produced."

As a survivor and as a witness, I was furious. I was not alone. Understandably, there was quite an outcry over the book, the article, and later Butz's website on the Internet. In an attempt to appease the critics, Northwestern University President Henry S. Bienen published a letter in which he said about Butz, "We can, and do, abhor the premise set forth in his book... Further, we recognize that Mr. Butz's expertise is in the fields of electrical engineering and computer science, and we are unaware of any academic credentials he has in history, sociology, or political science. (We) believe that his distortion of well-documented historical facts are a contemptible insult to all who experienced the horrors of that time, living and dead, to their families, and, indeed, to all of humanity." That said, he went on to defend intellectual freedom and freedom of speech.

I learned that Butz is on the editorial advisory committee of *The Journal of Historical Review*, published by the Institute for Historical Review (IHR). Historical review, journal, institute — these are lofty sounding names that conjure up images of academic and scholarly research. The IHR describes itself as "a not-for-profit research, educational, and publishing center devoted to truth and accuracy in history." Given this description, it would appear that the IHR pursues the worthy goal of examining the centuries of recorded history and pointing out possible weaknesses in the accounts.

On their website, they include a list of their pamphlets — a list that reveals the much narrower focus of the IHR's attention:

- A Few Facts About the IHR
- The "Problem of the Gas Chambers"
- Auschwitz Myths and Facts
- Let's Examine the Holocaust from All Sides
- The Liberation of the Camps
- What is "Holocaust Denial"?
- Inside the Auschwitz "Gas Chambers"
- Sixty-six Questions and Answers about the Holocaust
- The "Jewish Soap" Myth
- The U.S. Holocaust Memorial Museum
- Simon Wiesenthal: Bogus Nazi Hunter
- A Prominent False Witness: Elie Wiesel

Still, I asked myself, am I overreacting? Isn't it possible that these people are guilty only of benign ignorance? I wish that were true. Quite the contrary. Many of these folks are aggressively peddling their lies and, in doing so, are targeting the youth.

Deborah Lipstadt, in her book *Denying the Holocaust: The Growing Assault on Truth and Memory* (Plume, 1994) wrote that in the early 1990s, Holocaust deniers began focusing on American college campuses. According to Lipstadt, "Bradley Smith, a Californian who has been involved in a variety of Holocaust denial activities since the early 1980s, attempted to place a full-page ad claiming that the Holocaust was a hoax in college newspapers through the United States." The ad ran in the newspapers of such institutions as Cornell, Duke, Northwestern, Ohio State, Rutgers, and Vanderbilt. Whether or not the ad was accepted (some college papers chose not to accept his money, but ran the ad for discussion purposes), it generated a flurry of editorials, articles, and letters to editors that equated to millions of dollars in free publicity for Smith and his cause.

In an admitted publicity stunt in 1979, the IHR offered $50,000 to anyone who could prove that Jews were indeed killed in gas chambers by the Nazis. The promotion was a flop until the IHR mailed notices of the contest to several well-known Holocaust survivors. The entries, the rules said, would be judged by a panel appointed by the IHR. One of the flyers was sent to Mel Mermelstein of California, with a note stating that if he declined to participate, the IHR would publicize his refusal as undeniable proof that the Holocaust could not be substantiated. Mermelstein accepted the challenge on the condition that a judge appointed by the California Supreme Court determine the validity of his entry. The IHR declined, and Mermelstein sued for the full $50,000. The court decided in his favor and added another $40,000 to compensate Mermelstein for his pain and suffering.

So what is it that the revisionists and deniers of the Holocaust claim? Here are just a few of their assertions. The responses were prepared by The Simon Wiesenthal Center, of Los Angeles, California, and are reprinted here with permission:

The Holocaust was merely Allied propaganda.

The Allies actually ignored reports filtering out of Europe about the mass murder of Jews by the Nazis and their collaborators. Even when convinced of their veracity, they tried to withhold the information from the public. If the Holocaust were merely 'propaganda,' why did the Allies go to such lengths to downplay it?

There is no proof that the Holocaust occurred.

No crime in history has been as well documented as the Holocaust. Proof of the Holocaust is multi-faceted. It is demonstrated by a myriad of documents, the majority of them Nazi-authored, captured by Allied troops before the Germans had a chance to destroy them. Included are detailed reports of mass shootings and gassings.

The estimates of Jewish losses during the Holocaust are greatly exaggerated. There were never even six million Jews in Germany.

It is true that Germany had fewer than 600,000 Jews when Hitler came to power in 1933. The majority of Jews murdered by the Nazis, however, did not live in Germany. They resided in the countries which Germany invaded during the war. In fact, the Protocol of the Wannsee Conference (January 20, 1942), a German document outlining the Nazi plan to annihilate European Jewry, lists over 11 million Jews throughout the continent. Authentic German documents confirm the slaughter of Jews in the millions. The famous "Korherr

Report," (named after Richard Korherr, chief statistician for the SS) puts the number of Jewish losses at more than 2,454,000 by the end of 1942 alone.

Nazi policy towards the Jews was emigration, not extermination.
From the beginning, the Nazis made no secret of their goal of creating a "Jew-free" Germany and Europe. One of the earliest methods was, indeed, forced emigration. But on November 10, 1941, precise instructions from Berlin to kill the Jews in his area were received by the Higher SS and police leader Friedrich Jeckeln from Berlin, stating, that pursuant to the Fuehrer's order, Jews would no longer be allowed "to emigrate." Instead they would be "evacuated." In his October 4, 1943 speech to SS generals in Poznan, SS Chief Heinrich Himmler left no doubt as to the meaning of evacuation. "I am now referring to the evacuation of the Jews, the extermination of the Jewish people," he declared.

Zyklon B was a fumigant. It wasn't a practical agent for mass murder.
Ordinarily, Zyklon B (a hydrogen cyanide preparation) was used as an insecticide. Hydrogen cyanide, however, is actually more dangerous to humans than insects. When the level reaches only 300 parts per million, it will kill a person within a few minutes. Because Zyklon B was, in fact, so toxic, its manufacturers warned personnel not to reenter a room fumigated with the gas for 20 hours after airing. In addition, a compound was added to the preparation emitting a powerful, intolerable odor (a warning agent that the gas was present). When purchasing Zyklon B for the death camps, the SS ordered the manufacturer to remove the warning compound, a clear indication of its intended use. The death chambers were outfitted with special ventilation systems to remove any remaining gas. In addition, those prisoners charged with removing the bodies (the Sonderkommando) wore gas masks.

There is no proof whatsoever that the Nazis ever murdered anyone in gas chambers.
The use of gas chambers by the Nazis is proven by a wide array of evidence. Testimony by the perpetrators themselves as well as the firsthand accounts of prisoners, especially members of the Sonderkommando, constitute only a part of the evidence. Documents,

including blueprints of the killing installations as well as orders for construction materials and Zyklon B, survived the war as did some of the actual gassing facilities themselves.

American engineer and execution "expert" Fred Leuchter proved that the so-called gas chambers at Auschwitz could not have been used for their alleged purpose.

In 1988, Fred Leuchter, of Massachusetts, was contacted by Holocaust denier Robert Faurisson and hired to prepare a report on the gas chambers of Auschwitz on behalf of neo-Nazi Ernst Zundel. Zundel was on trial on charges stemming from the distribution of Holocaust revisionist literature. Leuchter visited the sites of the Auschwitz-Birkenau and Majdanek death camps. Upon returning to the United States, he published a lengthy report which concluded that the facilities he examined "could not have then been...utilized or seriously considered to function as execution gas chambers." During the trial, it was discovered that Leuchter had no credentials as an engineer... Judge Ronald Thomas listened to excerpts from the "Leuchter Report," then castigated the author for his methodology which he labeled "preposterous," ruling that "Leuchter has no expertise."

Later, Leuchter, who had represented himself as an engineer and execution expert to various government agencies for years, was indicted by the state of Massachusetts for posing as an engineer. As part of a pre-trial agreement, he admitted that he had never been a registered engineer and agreed to cease and desist from the distribution of any more engineering reports during his probationary period. Despite his embarrassment, Leuchter took his show to Germany. Arrested in October 1993 on charges of inciting racial hatred, he was released on bail and allowed to return to the U.S. pending trial. Leuchter, however, refused to return to Germany for trial.

The freedom of speech enjoyed by citizens of the United States, including Butz, Smith, Leuchter, and others who would skew the facts of history, is not shared across the world. In July 1998, *USA Today* reported that Swiss author Juergen Graf and his publisher were sentenced to prison for fifteen months and one year, respectively, for writing and distributing several books that denied the existence of Nazi gas chambers. Graf and Gerhard Foerster, a former Nazi officer,

were convicted of breaking Switzerland's law against racial
discrimination.

Hatred and Bigotry

But again, I have to ask myself, are these people who would
desecrate the memory of so many lives lost nothing more than
misguided individuals who can cause no real harm? One need not
look far to find the answer. There is a proliferation of groups spewing
venom of hatred and violence that base their doctrines, at least in
part, on the so-called teachings of the deniers and the revisionists.

The Ku Klux Klan, Aryan Nation, National Alliance, neo-Nazis,
White Power skinheads, National Social White Peoples Party, and
others espouse doctrines hauntingly reminiscent of those of Hitler.

The Aryan Nation, which prominently advertises for sale Henry Ford's
The International Jew and uses the swastika as one of its symbols, proclaims:

> We believe that the Cananite Jew is the natural enemy
> of our Aryan (White) Race. This is attested by scripture
> and all secular history. The Jew is like a destroying virus
> that attacks our racial body to destroy our Aryan culture....
>
> We, the remnant of the Aryan Race, shall again
> remove the blind fear that binds us in the cesspool of Jewry
> and acknowledge that we are in a state of war individually
> and collectively, and that there exists no common judge
> on earth to whom we can appeal. The Jews who have
> come in amongst us have not only evidenced a "sedate
> settled design" upon our lives but openly carry out the
> killing of members of our racial household and the looting
> of our property and sustenance.

Oddly, the Aryan Nation preaches a sermon of "love." This from
one of their publications:

> What is the actual driving force behind the 'racist'
> White Christian Nationalist's fight for the preservation of
> the Aryan Race? ....those long standing warriors in this
> Struggle know that the answer has a much greater depth
> and meaning than the anti-Christ Jews, mongrel hordes,
> and liberal White race-mixers could even begin to
> fathom...that of LOVE. The depths of Love are rooted
> and very deep in a real White Nationalist's soul and spirit,
> no form of "hate" could even begin to compare.

The Ku Klux Klan, whose membership requirements allow "only pure white Christian people of non-Jewish, non-Negro, non-Asian descent," states:

> The Knights of the Ku Klux Klan does not consider itself the enemy of non-Whites. The only way all races can develop their full potential and culture is through racial separation. ...The Klan will oppose integration and all its manifestations including affirmative action, the high-non-White crime rate, racial intermarriage, the destruction of our schools, lowering of labor standards, etc.

The National Alliance has similarly stringent membership rules:

> Any White person (a non-Jewish person of wholly European ancestry of good character and at least 18 years of age who accepts as his own the goals of the National Alliance...no homosexual or bisexual person, no person actively addicted to alcohol or to an illegal drug, no person with a non-White spouse or a non-White dependent, and, except in extraordinary circumstances, no person currently confined in a penal institution may be a member.

So what are the "goals" of the leaders and followers of the National Alliance? In their own words:

> We must have new societies throughout the White world which are based on Aryan values and are compatible with the Aryan nature. We do not need to homogenize the White world.... What we must have...is a thorough rooting out of Semitic and other non-Aryan values and customs everywhere. We must once again provide the sort of social and spiritual environment in which our own nature can express itself in music, in art and architecture, in literature, in philosophy and scholarship, in the mass media, and in the life-styles of the people.

The National Social White Peoples Party highlights the following pledge on its Internet radio show:

> I pledge allegiance to Adolph Hitler
> The immortal Leader of our race
> And to the New Order for which he stands
> One Great Cause, Sacred and Invincible
> The hope and future, of all Aryan man.
> Heil Hitler!

Although each of these groups will disclaim any involvement or any responsibility, the rise in hate crimes worldwide is undeniable. Here are just a few recent news reports:

Washington Post Foreign Service (March 5, 1998)

EBERSWALDE, GERMANY — Alarmed by the resurgence in right-wing extremism, the state of Brandenburg, which surrounds Berlin, has mobilized a 45-member commando squad to respond to emergency calls about neo-Nazi attacks. The rapid-reaction force, equipped with helicopters, special weapons, and high-speed vehicles, arrested 23 people in its first week of operations. ....German authorities say statistics tell only part of the story. They contend that right-wing groups are becoming increasingly dangerous because of more effective recruiting methods, improved organizational skills, computer websites that disseminate neo-Nazi propaganda and, most ominously, the firepower of their weapons.

Associated Press (April 19, 1998)

MINNEAPOLIS — A neo-Nazi rally turned violent Saturday as protesters threw rocks and insults at the group and took chains and poles to one of the organizers' cars. Eleven members of the National Socialist Movement arrived for a noon rally in downtown St. Paul and were met by about 20 protesters chanting "No Nazis, no killers." ....Swastika-emblazoned literature mailed out by the group condemned Jews and "coloreds" and advertised the event as the "Adolph Hitler Memorial Rally."

Associated Press (May 6, 1998)

BERLIN — ....The extreme-right has been gaining ground across Europe, playing on anti-foreigner sentiments. But the trend is especially disturbing in Germany, given its Nazi past. Some seek to explain the far right's resurgence in Germany as a protest against 12 percent unemployment. But others see a deeper problem developing that threatens to split society, especially in the east, where democratic traditions are still unformed after decades of communist rule.

Associated Press (May 6, 1998)

BONN — Right-wing attacks in Germany reached a three-year high in 1997, part of a broad resurgence of rightist extremism, a government report said today. It was the first increase in far-right violence since 1992, fueled in part by a growing racist music scene and a rising number of young Germans ready to vent rage through aggression.

Associated Press (May 25, 1998)

MOSCOW — At a recent gathering of veterans to celebrate the defeat of Nazi Germany and remember Russians' terrible suffering in World War II, a young man was busy handing out neo-Nazi propaganda. Nobody objected. ....In the past few months, Moscow has been the scene of an increasing number of racist attacks by skinheads, drawing attention to a small but violent neo-fascist movement. ...Some anti-fascists fear that the extremist view is gaining favor among some low-level officials, including the police.

An Observation

The Holocaust did not arise from nothing. It was not the result of one madman. For the Holocaust to have been possible, hatred of the Jews had to have been incubating for thousands of years, and that hatred had to be ignored by others during that time. That spark of hatred is still present, waiting to be fanned again into flames. There are tens of thousands of people organized across the world prepared and eager to do so today. All of humanity must be made aware of this. We must identify them, and we must hold them personally accountable as accessories, if not the perpetrators, for every act of hatred, for every incident of harassment or violence against anyone whether based on religion, the color of skin, national or ethnic differences, sexual preference, or difference in beliefs.

We need to educate ourselves and our children that, especially in times of social unrest (*e.g.*, high unemployment, financial depression, etc.), there are those who will attempt to seize power by spreading even further unrest. They will divert attention from the underlying causes of the unrest, and perhaps from their own shortcomings, by finding scapegoats they can blame. Most often the scapegoats are those in the minority. Too frequently, someone will propose the most expedient route to a better society is to exterminate the scapegoats.

Also to be remembered is the repeated lesson of history, that the killing of Jews is too often the beginning of a time of overall violence.

Once the task of killing the Jews was finished, Hitler's own plan called for the eventual annihilation of all "inferior" subject peoples — Jehovah's Witnesses, homosexuals, disabled people, the mentally ill and retarded, Gypsies, and indeed all religions. If only those who believed that the Jews were the sole intended victims could have realized that the Jewish people were only at the top of a much longer list that included them as well.

Eleven million innocent people were murdered by the Nazi barbarians, six million of whom were Jews. Eleven million was not a number. Each one was a life.

First They Came For...

In Germany, the Nazis first came for the communists, and I didn't speak up because I wasn't a communist.

Then they came for the Jews, and I didn't speak up because I wasn't a Jew.

Then they came for the trade unionists, and I didn't speak up because I wasn't a trade unionist.

Then they came for the Catholics, but I didn't speak up because I was a Protestant.

Then they came for me, and by that time there was no one left to speak for me.

By the Reverend Martin Niemoeller
(Reverend Niemoeller, a German Lutheran pastor, was arrested by the Nazis and imprisoned Dauchau in 1938. He was eventually freed by the Allied Forces in 1945.)

Chapter 17

WILL YOU MAKE THE MUSIC?

A m I a bitter old Jew? No. Old, perhaps, and hopefully wiser, but not bitter. Still, there are many ways in which the Holocaust affected, and continues to affect, my life. My war experiences left me damaged both emotionally and physically. I have frequent nightmares. Due to lingering feelings of insecurity, I keep all the shades drawn and the doors locked. I still prefer to live in the middle of the block and avoid sitting on the aisle at the theater. I go to great lengths to avoid a sense of being unnecessarily exposed.

For religious reasons, my head is always covered with a yarmulke, yet I am never without a hat or a cap to cover the yarmulke when I am out in public. I still harbor the fear of anti-Semitism from my youth, more so because it is increasingly around us today.

There is the memory of gnawing hunger that returns still. Holocaust survivors often will take small bags of food when leaving home, even if just for a few hours. At a party or reception, they may save some tidbits from the buffet table for later. Although I have never acquired this habit, I understand it completely.

Not one week goes by that I do not dream that I am still in a concentration camp. I think about my parents and fantasize about how wonderful it would be if only they could see their grandchildren. In a few days, this pain subsides, only to return again. When there is a *simcha*, a happy occasion, I cannot enjoy it fully because my parents are not able to share it with me. These emotional pains will plague me until I die.

I frequently experience severe back pains, and I will always walk with a limp. Naturally, I complain. But when I do, I ask myself, "Am I not much better off than those who did not survive?" The answer is a sobering and constant reminder of my good fortune.

I was liberated by the Russians in 1945, but I was not free. I and the others who survived were too weak and too mentally drained to rejoice. We realized that we were alone. We had lost our families, our friends, our homes, the countries of our births. The free world did not understand us, filled as we were with fears and emotional and physical trauma. The end of World War II was not the end of the Holocaust survivors' nightmare. Unfortunately, a large number could not face the realities of their renewed existence, and many lost faith in G-d and in humanity. Some committed suicide. We who survived were forced to live with memories that could never be fully described or understood. But instead of living in bitterness and hatred over the past fifty years, many have created a record of determination and accomplishment.

When you consider how many Holocaust survivors managed to put their shattered lives back together after the war and make significant contributions in art, music, theatre, literature, and to society in general, it is a true testament to the indomitability of the human spirit.

As is undoubtedly the case with all those who managed to emerge from the Nazi hell, not a day goes by that I do not think that for some reason, known only to G-d, I survived while most of those around me did not. Since I miraculously escaped the fires of the Holocaust, I could not be satisfied with merely surviving. I, too, had to do something meaningful with my life.

Am I a bitter old Jew? No, but I recognize that as a human being, it is my responsibility to make certain that the personal accounts of the survivors live on and to counter those who are trying to revise or deny the facts of the Holocaust. To do that, I remember those who so needlessly perished and speak out on their behalf. And, as a cantor and a rabbi, I try to reach into the hearts of all Jews wherever they are and rekindle within them the spark of Judaism.

One of the greatest lessons I learned from the Holocaust is an awareness of and appreciation for others and tolerance for all. And, because the human race seems plagued by an all-too-short memory, I've also learned that we need to remain ever vigilant.

A Parable

The parents of a young boy decided to place a nail in the door of their home every time the boy ignored or disobeyed them. Years passed, and the nails accumulated in the door. One day, the boy asked his parents what the nails meant, and his parents told him.

The father then made an offer. One nail would be removed for each good deed the boy performed. It took a couple of years, but the boy finally completed enough good deeds so that all the nails were gone. The family went out to a celebratory dinner.

"I'm so glad all the nails are gone," said the boy when the family returned home. But the father pointed to the door and asked his son to look more closely. "The holes will always remain there," he said.

❖❖❖

We must never forget the "holes." With the popularity of the U.S. Holocaust Memorial Museum in Washington, D.C., of the book and Steven Spielberg's film *Schindler's List*, and of other similar programs that have aired on television, we run the risk that people may want to congratulate themselves saying, "Finally, the Holocaust has been fully and adequately explained. Nothing more needs to be said or done. Let's put it behind us and move on." Nothing could be further from the truth. To be truly successful, the task will never be finished. It is not sufficient that the Holocaust has reached a peak of current public interest. In fact, it is more necessary than ever that the message continues to be told in a manner that is both correct and constructive.

People have to understand that those who stand in silence when a crime is committed share in the guilt for that crime. Therefore, we must diligently strive to build a better society, for harmony even with people who are different from us or with whom we may disagree.

After the great flood, G-d said, "My rainbow I place in the clouds, and it will be a sign of my covenant with the earth." The rainbow symbolizes peace and unity. A rainbow is made up of many colors which, although they are very different from one another, blend together to create one incredible picture. People, too, are very different from one another. We all come from assorted national backgrounds and religions and possess a limitless number of personalities. But if we will only look at ourselves as the one body of humanity that we truly are, there can be peace and harmony despite our differences. It is essential for the existence of the world and for the welfare of all individuals that we do so.

Will we ever learn? When things are going well in our lives, we tend to take everything for granted, and we forget to thank G-d for His blessings. When things turn against us, we repeatedly vow to lead more ethical lives, only to return to our old ways when the situation improves. The following story illustrates this all-too-human tendency.

A rabbi visited a man in the hospital. The sick man begged the rabbi to pray for his recovery, pledging $10,000 to the synagogue once he was well. The rabbi made a special prayer on his behalf, and soon the man returned home in good health. Some time later, the rabbi reminded the man of his promise. "Did I really say $10,000?" he asked.

"Yes, you did," answered the rabbi.

"Well, you can see, that only shows you how sick I was!"

G-d acts in mysterious ways. We are people who believe in miracles. Our very survival of the Holocaust cannot be explained other than as a miracle, even if it embarrasses us to admit it. Why did G-d, who created so many miracles during the time of the Bible, apparently stop performing them during the Holocaust? And why isn't He performing them to alleviate the pain and suffering in the world today? One noted rabbi remarked, "There are miracles under your chair if only you will bend down to pick them up." Increasingly, we seem unwilling to bend down. We must recognize them for what they are. Life itself is a miracle.

In recent years, there have been several books published that speculate on what happens to the human spirit after death. Humankind has grappled with the mysteries surrounding death since earliest recorded times, and probably for a long time before that. Some of these books have dealt with interviews of those who have clinically died, only to be resuscitated. In a striking number of these instances, those interviewed reported a feeling of being embraced by a bright light that they could only describe as pure and omniscient love.

Perhaps most important is that nearly all of the subjects said they brought back with them to this life the singular message that the only thing that truly matters is love. Nothing else is important. It's interesting to note that these people, and there have been thousands of such cases documented, represent many different nations and many differenxt faiths. Some of those who "died" had even lived their lives professing to be atheists, only to return from death either convinced there is indeed a G-d, or at least that there is an afterlife.

While I'm not at all certain that I accept as unquestionably valid these reported experiences, I'm old enough and have certainly witnessed a sufficient number of unbelievable things in my life to know that I should at least listen. What gets my attention is the universal theme that, in the final analysis, *love is all there is.*

Other books have been written about certain people who appear to be attuned to the spirits of those who have passed away. James Van Praagh is one who has attained worldwide fame for his apparent ability to communicate with those no longer with us. Again, I don't necessarily subscribe to the belief that people can actually communicate with the dead; there is, however, the recurring theme that love is the only universal and all-important commodity of our existence. That intrigues me. In his recent book *Talking to Heaven* (NAL/Dutton, 1998), Van Praagh writes:

> We are *all* the same. G-d has *not* chosen one group above another. When we dare to be aware, we will raise our understanding and compassion and see everyone as part of the universal energy of G-d. We will be free of prejudice and hatred based on someone's color, race, sex, or gender preference. G-d is not limited. Only humans limit their thinking. ...Ultimately, it is up to us as individuals to know that our worth and value cannot be measured by any amount of money that we may have in the bank, or the size of our house, or the number of cars we own. When we pass to the other side, the only question we will be asked has to do with the *amount of love* we have in our hearts.

If I have touched even one person by sharing what I endured, then I have returned something for the love and life I received from G-d. We need to remember that we are never totally alone, for G-d is always with us. Patience, tolerance, faith, and love will see us through anything. In addition to learning to believe in myself, I know that when I reach out to G-d, He will meet me halfway. Events in my life show that He is always guiding me. I am alive because G-d watched over me. He did not fail me, although I have no doubt failed Him at times.

When you are forced to crawl through a dark tunnel of depression and hardship, you must find the strength to persevere. Why? Because it's always possible the sun is shining on the other side! I sincerely believe we who survived the Holocaust had to endure our "dark tunnel" to help make this world a better and sunnier place.

It is of utmost importance that we work together to rid the world of bigotry and to promote acceptance. Everyone has a right to his or her own opinion. We must not, however, impose our beliefs on others. We should accept people the way they are, not the way we want them to be. Further, we must not be afraid to disagree, for the majority is not always right. It is our duty to speak out when we witness an injustice. And we need to challenge those who preach hatred of any kind.

Educate yourself and form your own opinions. The Holocaust did not happen suddenly. It started insidiously, step by step. To prevent another Holocaust, we have to stop hatred dead in its tracks. How?

We must teach others what can happen when we care only about ourselves. It says in the Hebrew Bible, *"V'ahavta l'reecha kamokha"* — *Love thy neighbor as thyself.* I searched to see if it said *Love thy Jewish neighbor* or *Love thy Black neighbor* or *Love thy Christian neighbor* or *Love thy Muslim neighbor.* It does not say that. It says quite simply, *Love thy neighbor.* You are my neighbor. And I am yours.

Am I a bitter old Jew? No, I am quite joyful and optimistic; and, in the scope of history, I am a young Jew — a young Jew who recognizes that the key to peace the world over is education and communication. I am aware that we must all work together for better human tolerance and understanding. There are many religions in the world, and all worship the same G-d. The only difference is that we reach this one G-d through different channels. Different channels, the same G-d. I try to teach others what channel Jews use and to learn and appreciate which ones they use.

A variety of instruments working in harmony are required to create an orchestra. For the sake of the world and future generations, we need to create a beautiful human orchestra that produces a symphony of love and acceptance. Let us each, regardless of race or religion, pick up the instruments of love within our hearts and contribute our own music to a better world. Our ultimate survival and eternal happiness depend upon it.

Notes

I changed my name to Leo when I became a Canadian citizen. Dezso changed his to Daniel, and we now call him Danny, and his wife, Marika, changed hers to Margie.

Danny opened his own supermarket in Indiana. In time, he became quite a successful business executive. Margie and Danny have four children and nine grandchildren. They now live in Lincolnwood, Illinois, and winter in Miami Beach, Florida.

The Nazis were constantly taking photographs. Years after the war, I discovered a very special picture. It was taken just minutes after we got off the train in Auschwitz. It shows my father and brother. I was next to my father, but I am not in the picture. This photograph is the one I chose for the cover of this book, and it is this picture that my grandson Yoni wrote about in the foreword to this book. I first found this picture in a book about the Holocaust. I took this book with me when I visited my brother in Chicago, I told him, "Danny, open this book. Look over the pages." When he came across this photograph, he stopped momentarily and then went on. "Look at it again," I told him. Then I asked him, "Danny, don't you know who this is?"

"Of course, I do."

"Then why did you skip by it?"

"I was not in Auschwitz," he answered. "I didn't know how you felt about the picture and didn't want to stir up bad memories."

Cantor Fettman and his granddaughter, Fraidel, in front of the photograph in Yad Vashem, the Holocaust museum in Jerusalem, 1998.

Our eldest daughter, Aviva, is married to Rabbi Joel Schwab of Temple Sinai in Middletown, New York, where she teaches a course called S.T.E.P. (Systematic Training for Effective Parenting). Their son, Yoni, is in his third year at Columbia University. Their other son, Ami, is currently studying in Jerusalem and will enter Columbia University in 1999. Both young men are also enrolled in the Jewish Theological Seminary.

Renana is the family calligrapher and lives in Cincinnati, Ohio, where she works as a surveyor. Miriam is married to Yaakov Berger, and they live in Rochester, New York, where she works in the library system. Martin lives in Phoenix, Arizona, with five cats and a dog. He runs a business selling tickets to major sporting and entertainment events.

Jack manages an electronic department service. He and his wife, Esther Malka, live in Brooklyn, New York, with their three daughters, Atarah, Yehudis, and Tehila Bracha. Rachel is married to a dentist, Dr. Chaim Heifetz, and lives in Har Nof, Jerusalem. Chaim is also enrolled in advanced Torah studies at the yeshiva. They have two sons, Yosef and Nissy, and two daughters, Chavie and Bracha Fraidel.

ABOUT LEO & ANNETTE

Cantor Leo Fettman was born in Hungary in 1925. He began his religious education at an early age and attended Rabbinical Yeshiva in Hungary. In 1944, he was taken to Auschwitz along with his family, most of whom were killed there. He survived the Holocaust and eventually immigrated to Canada. He studied at the Maor Hagolah Rabbinical Yeshiva in Montreal, where he was ordained as rabbi and cantor. He studied at McGill University, Franconita Music School, and the University of Wisconsin.

Cantor Fettman has served as cantor for the High Holidays in cities in Europe, Canada, and the United States. He served as cantor and teacher, as well as a hospital chaplain, in Madison, Wisconsin, from 1963 to 1975, after which he was hired as cantor for the Beth Israel Synagogue in Omaha, Nebraska.

In Omaha, he served not only as cantor, but as the director of education, Shabbatonim developer and director, director and teacher of classes for Jews by Choice, and has provided kashrut supervision for the community. He is a widely-traveled speaker on the subject of Holocaust.

Cantor Fettman is listed in *Who's Who in Religion, Who's Who in the Midwest,* and in *Who's Who in Wisconsin.*

Annette Fettman was born in Chicago, Illinois, in 1925. She received a BA in Art from the University of Wisconsin in Madison. She continued her studies at the Chicago Academy of Fine Arts, UCLA, Madison Area Technical College, Creighton University, and Bellevue University.

She works in terra cotta and, in 1976, began experimenting with bronze sculpture, combining this with the theme of the Holocaust. She said about the Holocaust, "Inhumanity is so foreign to my nature that I must visually express man's inhumanity to man so that I, myself, can comprehend the suffering and terrible destruction of the period." She recently held her first one-person show at the Jewish Community Center Gallery.